United States Government Accountability Office

GAO

Report to the Ranking Member,
Committee on the Judiciary
U.S. Senate

February 2012

WHISTLEBLOWER PROTECTION

Actions Needed to Improve DOD's Military Whistleblower Reprisal Program

GAO
Accountability ★ Integrity ★ Reliability

GAO-12-362

G A O
Accountability * Integrity * Reliability

Highlights

Highlights of GAO-12-362, a report to the Ranking Member, Committee on the Judiciary, U. S. Senate

WHISTLEBLOWER PROTECTION

Actions Needed to Improve DOD's Military Whistleblower Reprisal Program

Why GAO Did This Study

Whistleblowers help guard the federal government against waste, fraud, and abuse. The Military Whistleblower Protection Act provides servicemembers with a means to seek relief from reprisals and to hold subjects accountable. GAO was asked to determine the extent to which the Department of Defense (DOD) has (1) satisfied statutory timeliness requirements for processing military whistleblower reprisal cases, (2) established and implemented oversight mechanisms for its process, and (3) taken corrective action in cases where the DOD Inspector General (DODIG) substantiated reprisal claims. GAO also analyzed case characteristics. GAO examined laws, regulations, and guidance documents; interviewed officials from DODIG, service IGs, service Boards for the Correction of Military Records (BCMRs), and the Office of the Undersecretary of Defense for Personnel and Readiness; and collected and analyzed case data. GAO also conducted a detailed file review using a representative sample of cases closed between January 1, 2009 and March 31, 2011.

What GAO Recommends

GAO recommends that DOD implement procedures to track and report data on its case processing timeliness, take actions to improve oversight of its investigative process, and develop processes to ensure appropriate corrective actions are taken in substantiated cases. DOD concurred with all of GAO's recommendations.

View GAO-12-362. For more information, contact Zina Merritt at (202) 512-5257 or merrittz@gao.gov.

What GAO Found

DODIG has taken multiple steps, in collaboration with the service IGs in some instances, to improve DOD's ability to process military whistleblower reprisal cases in a timely manner. Timeliness is important to ensure the reliability of evidence and appropriate resolution of reprisal allegations. However, DODIG has generally not met statutory requirements to report on investigations within 180 days, or to provide alternative notification. DODIG has undertaken efforts to improve timeliness by, for example, eliminating a time-consuming phase of its investigative process. However, DOD's efforts are hampered by unreliable and incomplete data. For instance, GAO found that DODIG has not consistently or accurately recorded key dates to track how long investigations take to complete. Without key timeliness data, DODIG may have difficulty in identifying process areas requiring improvement and evaluating the impact of reforms. Further, the absence of this information limits congressional decision makers' ability to provide oversight of DOD's whistleblower reprisal investigative program.

DODIG has begun executing an action plan that includes acting on prior external and internal review recommendations in order to improve its oversight of the department's whistleblower reprisal process, but implementation of this plan is not yet complete and challenges exist in three areas:

- *Performance metrics.* DODIG has not yet established performance metrics to ensure the quality of reprisal investigations.
- *Guidance.* DOD's guidance related to the whistleblower program is outdated and does not reflect current investigative processes. Additionally, some of the guidance is unclear, leading to inconsistent implementation among the service IGs. Moreover, DODIG has not been consistently adhering to standards regarding the maintenance of its case files, resulting in generally incomplete files.
- *Case monitoring processes and procedures.* DODIG lacks standard case monitoring processes and procedures, which may hinder its ability to consistently maintain visibility and assess the status of outstanding reprisal investigations including those conducted by service and component IGs.

Until it further addresses the challenges it faces in regard to oversight mechanisms, DODIG cannot be assured that it is effectively conducting its oversight responsibilities or implementing the whistleblower reprisal program as intended.

DOD's efforts to ensure that appropriate corrective action is taken—both for whistleblowers and against those who reprise against whistleblowers—are hampered by disconnected investigative and corrective action processes and the limited visibility of the corrective actions taken. DODIG and the service BCMRs are not consistently identifying and tracking data on action taken to undo the reprisal damage done to whistleblowers. Further, unreliable data regarding corrective action taken against those found to have reprised against whistleblowers is hindering oversight of this key aspect of whistleblower protections. Without addressing these issues, whistleblowers may not be getting the full protection and resolution they deserve.

_____ **United States Government Accountability Office**

Contents

Figures

United States Government Accountability Office
Washington, DC 20548

February 22, 2012

The Honorable Charles E. Grassley
Ranking Member, Committee on the Judiciary
United States Senate

Whistleblowers play an important role in safeguarding the federal government against waste, fraud, and abuse, and their willingness to come forward can contribute to improvements in government operations. These whistleblowers also risk reprisals from their employers, sometimes being demoted, reassigned, or fired. In 1988, Congress enacted the Military Whistleblower Protection Act,[1] which provides protections from reprisal for a servicemember who discloses information concerning, among other things, fraud, waste, and abuse to designated persons such as an inspector general (IG) or someone in the servicemember's chain of command.[2] Under this law, the Department of Defense (DOD) IG has final responsibility for approving the results of all investigations, although both DODIG and the service IGs can investigate allegations of reprisal.[3]

---

[1] National Defense Authorization Act, Fiscal Year 1989, Pub. L. No. 100-456, §846 (1988), codified at 10 U.S.C. § 1034, as amended.

[2] Specifically, 10 U.S.C. § 1034 prohibits individuals from restricting a member of the armed forces (hereafter referred to as servicemember) from making a lawful communication to a Member of Congress or an Inspector General (IG). It further prohibits individuals from taking or threatening to take an unfavorable personnel action, or withholding or threatening to withhold a favorable personnel action, as a reprisal against a servicemember for making or preparing to make a lawful communication to a Member of Congress or an IG or from communicating to a Member of Congress, IG, a member of a Department of Defense audit, inspection, investigation, or law enforcement organization; any person or organization in the chain of command; or any other person or organization designated pursuant to regulations or other established administrative procedures for such communications regarding what the servicemember reasonably believes to be evidence of any of the following: a violation of law or regulation, including a law or regulation prohibiting sexual harassment or unlawful discrimination, gross mismanagement, a gross waste of funds, an abuse of authority, or a substantial and specific danger to public health or safety.

[3] Department of Defense Directive 7050.06, *Military Whistleblower Protection* (Jul. 23, 2007) defines the military department.IGs as including the IG of the Army, the Naval IG, the IG of the Air Force, and the Deputy Naval IG for Marine Corps Matters (Marine Corps IG). In this report, we refer to these organizations collectively as the service IGs.

Despite the protections afforded to military whistleblowers under the Military Whistleblower Protection Act and subsequent amendments, concerns persisted that servicemembers were not being adequately protected by DOD's investigative process. In response, DODIG requested that the Department of Justice IG assess whether DODIG was properly and effectively discharging its statutory responsibilities to protect members of the Armed Forces from reprisal.[4] The resulting July 2009 report[5] highlighted timeliness in processing complaints as DOD's biggest challenge and made detailed recommendations for improvement based on the underlying report findings.

To assist Congress in providing oversight of DOD's efforts to protect military whistleblowers, you asked us to examine DOD's military whistleblower reprisal process. Specifically, this report examines the extent to which DOD has (1) satisfied statutory timeliness requirements for processing military whistleblower reprisal cases and what factors, if any, impact its ability to do so; (2) established and implemented oversight mechanisms for its military whistleblower reprisal process; and (3) taken corrective action in cases where DODIG substantiated military whistleblower reprisal claims. The report also identifies key characteristics of military whistleblower reprisal cases.

To address these objectives, we reviewed a random selection of case files retained by DODIG for military whistleblower reprisal cases closed between January 1, 2009 and March 31, 2011, to identify case characteristics, and address the extent to which DODIG met timeliness

---

[4] The Department of Justice IG review examined: (1) the statute and DOD regulations relating to military whistleblowers; (2) the allocation of responsibility for conducting investigations of military whistleblower reprisal allegations among the DODIG and the service IGs; (3) the management, staffing, and processes of the DODIG directorate responsible for military whistleblower reprisal investigations; (4) the quality of DODIG's investigative product and its oversight of the service IGs' processing and investigation of reprisal complaints; and (5) the effectiveness of DODIG in satisfying its legal obligations and ensuring that reprisal allegations are thoroughly and fairly investigated.

[5] U.S. Department of Justice, Office of the Inspector General, *A Review of the Department of Defense Office of Inspector General's Process for Handling Military Whistleblower Reprisal Allegations* (July 2009).

requirements and had oversight mechanisms in place.[6] The margin of error associated with the confidence intervals of our case file review proportion estimates is no more than plus or minus 11 percentage points at the 95 percent level of confidence. The margin of error for any mean values based on our case file review will vary depending on the variability of the data and so is reported along with the mean. To address all our audit objectives, we also collected and analyzed data on all closed military whistleblower reprisal cases from DODIG,[7] the headquarters-level IGs from the Army, Navy, Air Force, and Marine Corps,[8] and the Boards for Correction of Military Records (BCMRs) of the Army, Navy,[9] and Air Force.[10] We assessed the data we obtained and determined that the data we used were sufficiently reliable for our audit objectives. We also reviewed relevant laws, regulations and guidance documents, internal memos, reports, and briefings. Further, we interviewed officials from DODIG, the service headquarters IGs and service field IGs from the Army, Navy, Air Force, and Marine Corps, and the Army, Navy, and Air Force BCMRs, as well as the Office of the Under Secretary of Defense for Personnel and Readiness – Enterprise Services. We conducted this performance audit from April 2011 to February 2012 in accordance with generally accepted government auditing standards. Those standards require that we plan and perform the audit to obtain sufficient, appropriate evidence to provide a reasonable basis for our findings and conclusions based on our audit objectives. We believe that the evidence obtained provides a reasonable basis for our findings and conclusions based on our audit objectives. Additional details on our scope and methodology are discussed in more detail in appendix I.

---

[6] We selected a random sample of 97 cases from a list provided by DODIG of a total of 871 military whistleblower reprisal cases closed between January 1, 2009 and March 31, 2011. However, we had to exclude 6 cases from our analyses because they were not accurately characterized in DODIG's database. Specifically, 3 cases were ongoing investigations, 2 cases were not military whistleblower reprisal cases, and DODIG could not locate 1 case file.

[7] Data from DODIG were for all military whistleblower reprisal cases closed between fiscal year 2006 and the first half of fiscal year 2011 (October 1, 2005 through March 31, 2011).

[8] Data from the service IGs were for all military whistleblower reprisal cases closed between January 1, 2009 and March 31, 2011.

[9] The Navy's BCMR also reviews cases brought to it by members of the Marine Corps.

[10] Data from the service BCMRs were for all military whistleblower reprisal cases closed by DODIG between fiscal year 2006 and the first half of fiscal year 2011.

Background

The Military Whistleblower Protection Act of 1988, as amended, and its implementing directive, Department of Defense Directive 7050.06,[11] establish the basic concepts and framework for the investigative process and establish the roles and responsibilities of the various affected organizations. DODIG is the central organization for DOD's military whistleblower reprisal program and has a directorate responsible for investigations into military whistleblower reprisal allegations. This directorate also conducts or oversees investigations into allegations of improper referrals of servicemembers for mental health evaluations[12] and conducts investigations into reprisal allegations involving civilians, contractors, and nonappropriated fund employees,[13,14] although historically military whistleblower reprisal cases make up approximately 80 percent of its caseload. Under the law, the service IGs and other DOD component IGs[15] can also investigate military whistleblower reprisal allegations and make recommendations regarding the disposition of cases. However, DODIG is responsible for reviewing and approving the results of all investigations of military whistleblower reprisal allegations. DODIG publicly reports on its military whistleblower protection program activities in its required semiannual report to Congress, including consolidated data on all of the cases the reprisal directorate received and

---

[11] Department of Defense Directive 7050.06, *Military Whistleblower Protection* (Jul. 23, 2007).

[12] Allegations of an improper referral of a servicemember for a mental health evaluation are subject to different laws and regulations, although referrals for mental health evaluations are included in the definition of personnel action, for the purposes of alleging a reprisal under Department of Defense Directive 7050.06.

[13] A nonappropriated fund instrumentality (NAFI) employee is a civilian employee who is paid from nonappropriated funds of the Army and Air Force Exchange Service, Navy exchanges Service Command, Marine Corps exchanges, or any other instrumentality of the United States under the jurisdiction of the armed forces which is conducted for the comfort, pleasure, contentment, or physical or mental improvement of members of the armed forces.

[14] DODIG had a separate directorate to investigate whistleblower reprisal allegations filed by civilians, but this directorate was merged in October 2011 with the directorate responsible for whistleblower reprisal investigations for servicemembers (military whistleblower reprisal), contractors, and nonappropriated fund employees, as well as improper referrals of servicemembers for mental health evaluations.

[15] DOD Directive 7050.06 defines DOD components as including the following organizational entities: Office of the Secretary of Defense, the Military Departments, the Chairman of the Joint Chiefs of Staff, the Combatant Commands, DODIG, the Defense Agencies, the DOD Field Activities, and all other organizational entities within DOD.

closed—numbers that include military whistleblower reprisal cases.[16] A description of some of the key organizations and individuals and their roles in the military whistleblower reprisal process can be found in table 1.

---

[16] Section 5 of appendix 3 of Title 5 of the United States Code requires each inspector general to prepare semiannual reports summarizing the activities of the office during the immediately preceding 6-month period ending March 31 and September 30, no later than April 30 and October 31 of each year. The law specifies that the report is to include, among other things, a description of significant problems, abuses, and deficiencies relating to the administration of programs and operations of that establishment.

Table 1: Roles and Responsibilities of Key Organizations and Individuals in the Military Whistleblower Reprisal Process

Organization or individuals	Roles and responsibilities
Complainant	• Military member who alleges that they have been reprised against for their whistleblower activities.
Subject or Responsible Management Official	• Individual who is alleged to have reprised against a whistleblower.
Secretaries of the Military Departments	Responsible for: • Ensuring that consideration of all military whistleblower allegations submitted under the Military Whistleblower Protection Act are thorough, objective, and timely, and that corrective actions are taken promptly.
Department of Defense Inspector General (DODIG)	Responsible for: • Directly receiving some whistleblower reprisal complaints, expeditiously conducting investigations. • Providing management and oversight of all military whistleblower reprisal investigations conducted by other IGs in DOD and the whistleblower reprisal investigative process in general. • Reviewing and approving all determinations reached by service IGs in military whistleblower reprisal investigations.
Service Inspectors General (IGs)	Inspectors General from the military services (Army, Navy, Air Force, Marine Corps) are responsible for: • Notifying the DODIG within 10 working days of receiving any whistleblower reprisal allegation. • Receiving, expeditiously investigating, and, if they choose, making recommendations on case disposition to DODIG.
Boards for the Correction of Military Records (BCMR)[a]	Military department organizations (Army, Air Force, Navy) with responsibility for: • Reviewing and taking action on applications for the correction of military records at the request of a complainant (the secretary of the military department concerned issues the final decision on the application). • Requesting, if they deem it necessary, that DODIG or the service IGs gather further evidence.
Office of the Under Secretary of Defense for Personnel and Readiness – Enterprise Services[b]	Organization within the Department of Defense responsible for: • Receiving information on all IG military whistleblower reprisal investigations that exceed 180 days as well as the results of full investigations. • Reviewing and making final decisions on behalf of the Secretary of Defense on appeals of BCMR whistleblower reprisal decisions.

Source: GAO analysis of DOD information.

[a]The Navy BCMR also reviews cases brought to it by members of the Marine Corps.

bDOD Directive 7050.06 (Jul. 23, 2007) assigns responsibility for the noted functions to the Deputy Under Secretary of Defense for Program Integration. In July 2010, the Under Secretary of Defense for Personnel and Readiness began to reorganize and realign Program Integration. On December 1, 2011, the Office of the Under Secretary of Defense for Personnel and Readiness (OUSD(P&R)) - Enterprise Services was designated as the successor organization for the Deputy Under Secretary of Defense for Program Integration.

The two basic components of a whistleblower reprisal allegation are the protected communication and the unfavorable personnel action. A protected communication is any lawful communication to a Member of Congress or an IG or a communication with appropriate officials about information that the servicemember reasonably believes evidences a violation of law or regulation, including a law or regulation prohibiting sexual harassment or unlawful discrimination, gross mismanagement, a gross waste of funds or other resources, an abuse of authority, or a substantial and specific danger to public health or safety.[17] A servicemember who makes or prepares to make a protected communication is considered a whistleblower. It is DOD's policy that servicemembers shall be free from reprisal for making or preparing to make a protected communication and that no person may take or threaten to take an unfavorable personnel action, such as an unfavorable performance evaluation, or withhold or threaten to withhold a favorable personnel action, such as granting a promotion or award, in reprisal for making or preparing to make a protected communication.[18]

To initiate an investigation under the Military Whistleblower Protection Act, a servicemember must typically make a reprisal allegation to an IG in DOD within 60 days of becoming aware of the personnel action alleged to

[17] DOD Directive 7050.06 Section E2.9 defines protected communication and lists the appropriate officials as a Member of Congress, an IG, or a member of a DOD audit, inspection, investigation, or law enforcement organization, or any person or organization in the chain of command; or any other person designated pursuant to regulations or other established administrative procedures to receive such communications.

[18] DOD Directive 7050.06 Section E2.8 defines a personnel action as any action taken on a servicemember that affects, or has the potential to affect, that military member's current position or career. Such actions include a promotion; a disciplinary or other corrective action; a transfer or reassignment; a performance evaluation; a decision on pay, benefits, awards, or training; referral for mental health evaluations under DOD Directive 6490.1; and any other significant change in duties or responsibilities inconsistent with the military member's grade.

have been taken in reprisal.[19,20] Allegations can also come to an IG through a Member of Congress. Once a complaint has been filed, the investigating organization—typically a service IG or DODIG—conducts a review to determine if the complaint qualifies as a whistleblower reprisal under the law and should be fully investigated. DODIG can also assign cases it receives to a service or other component IG for investigation and will also investigate cases that were not filed with it if the case is of special interest to DODIG.[21] If a complaint is fully investigated, the investigating organization writes a formal report of investigation that includes a determination of whether the complaint is substantiated or not substantiated. Such a report also receives at least one legal sufficiency review. Complaints that are not fully investigated do not necessarily include a formal report or a legal review. No determination, including a determination that a complaint does not merit a full investigation, is final until DODIG approves it. Even after a full investigation is completed that substantiates reprisal, servicemembers do not receive relief from the unfavorable personnel actions from IGs in DOD but instead must separately apply to their military department's Board for Correction of Military Records (BCMR). See figure 1 for the process currently used by DOD to investigate military whistleblower reprisal allegations.

---

[19] Under 10 U.S.C. §1034 (c)(4) IGs at DOD are not required to investigate allegations that are made more than 60 days after the date the servicemember becomes aware of the unfavorable personnel action that is alleged to have occurred as a result of reprisal. According to Section E3.1.1 of DOD Directive 7050.06, while no investigation is required in those cases, an authorized IG receiving such a complaint may, nevertheless, consider the complaint based on compelling reasons for the delay in submission or the strength of the evidence submitted.

[20] 10 U.S.C. §1034 (i) also includes the Department of Homeland Security (DHS) IG as a qualifying IG, in the case of a member of the Coast Guard when the Coast Guard is not operating as a service in the Navy. According to DODIG officials, they do not have any record of a Coast Guard military whistleblower reprisal allegation and are not aware of any such complaints brought by a member of the Coast Guard to the DHS IG.

[21] DODIG officials told us that cases of special interest could include high-profile cases, including those with congressional interest and cases that involve a complainant from one service and a subject from another.

Figure 1: The Military Whistleblower Reprisal Investigative Process, as of January 2012

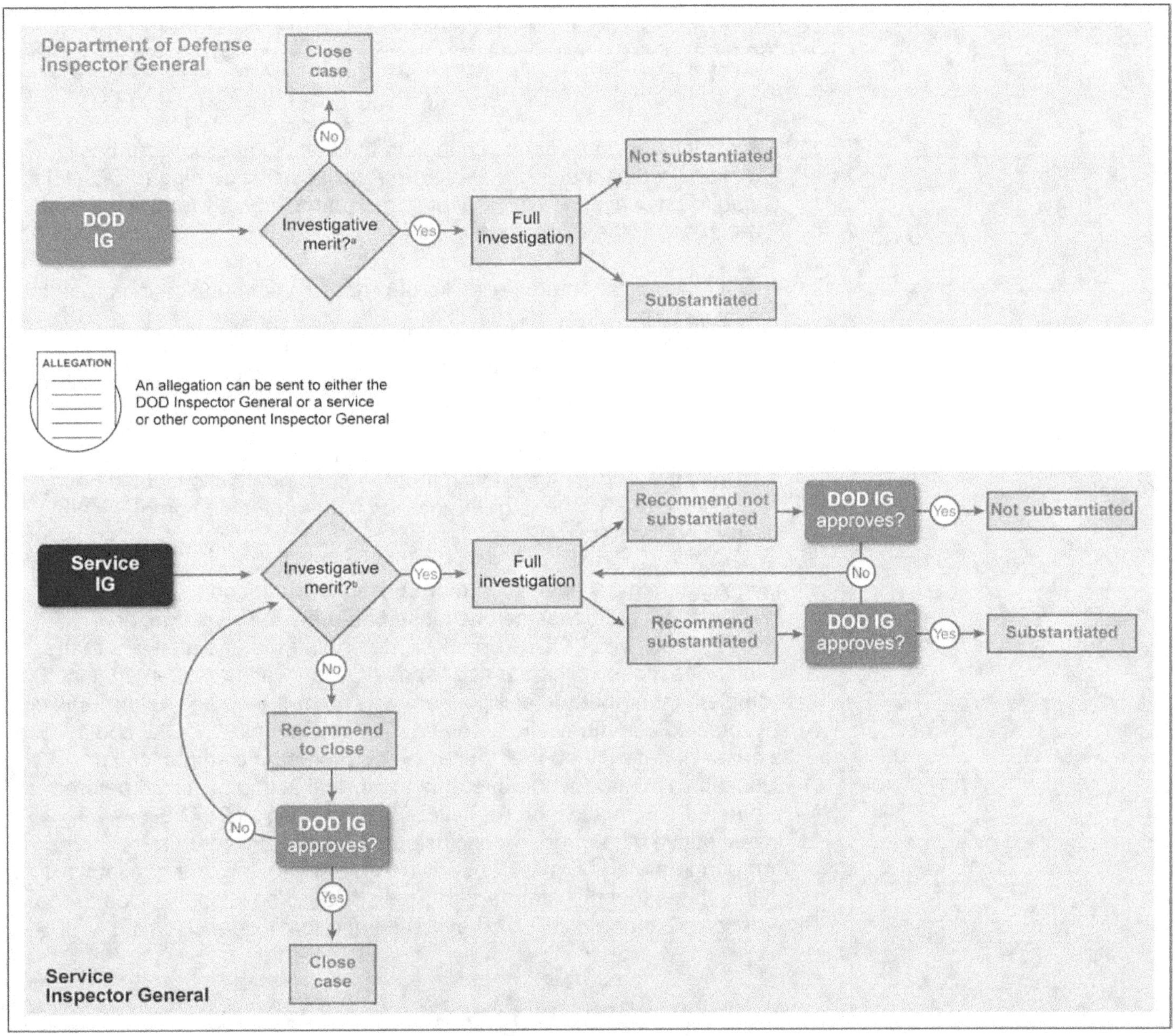

Source: GAO analysis of DOD information.

Notes:

Since 2008, cases filed by servicemembers in the Army have undergone an initial review of investigative merit by DODIG.

GAO-12-362 Whistleblower Protection

DODIG can also assign cases it receives to a service or component IG for investigation, and will also investigate cases that were not filed with it if the case is of special interest to DODIG.

[a]Currently, the determination of investigative merit by DODIG involves making an initial determination based on testimonial, and sometimes documentary evidence provided by the complainant.

[b]The determination of investigative merit for the service IGs spans a range and could be based on an assessment of the documents provided by the complainant but could also include a formal written report.

IGs at DOD assess each allegation in the complaint using four basic questions, which they refer to as the "Acid Test." According to DODIG's *Guide to Investigating Reprisal and Improper Referrals for Mental Health Evaluations,*[22] the four questions are:

1. Did the military member make or prepare a communication protected by statute?
2. Was an unfavorable personnel action taken or threatened, or was a favorable action withheld or threatened to be withheld following the protected communication?
3. Did the official(s) responsible for taking, withholding, or threatening the personnel action know about the protected communication?
4. Does the evidence establish that the personnel action would have been taken, withheld, or threatened if the protected communication had not been made?

Investigators must answer all four questions when conducting a full investigation, but cases can be closed before a full investigation if investigators, with DODIG approval, determine that the answers to the earlier questions indicate that a reprisal action was not taken against the complainant or that the complainant was not reprised against for making a protected communication (see fig. 2). For example, DODIG could close a case if it determined that there was no protected communication (question 1) or that an unfavorable personnel action occurred before the protected communication (question 2). According to DODIG's investigative guide, report conclusions are to be based on a "preponderance of the evidence" when assessing the four questions. The guide states that this standard requires that more weight is given to the most credible and convincing evidence and that evidence which

---

[22] DOD Inspector General Departmental Guidance 7050.6, *Guide to Investigating Reprisal and Improper Referrals for Mental Health Evaluations,* (Feb. 6, 1996). In this report we refer to this document as the DODIG investigative guide.

demonstrates to the reader that it is more probable than not that the facts and circumstances occurred as set forth in the investigative report.

Figure 2: Acid Test for Military Whistleblower Reprisal Allegations

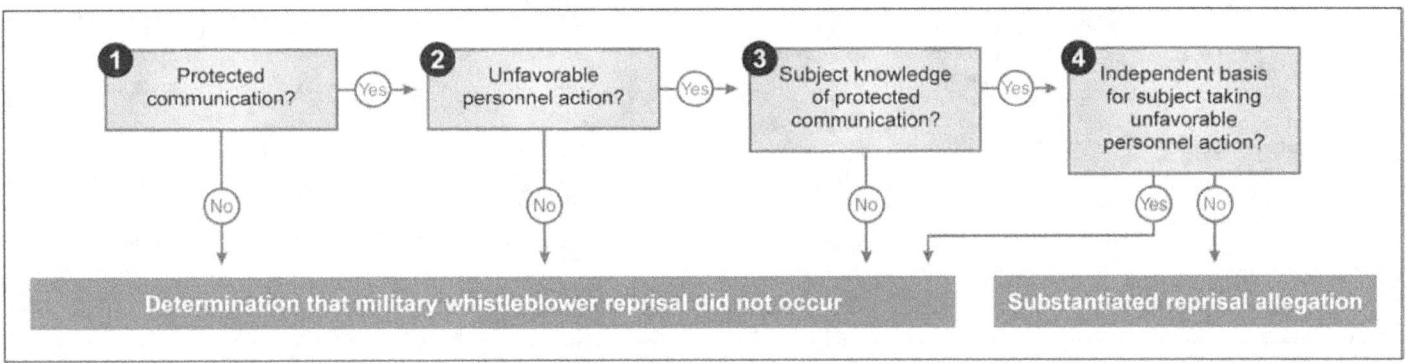

Source: GAO analysis of DOD information.

Although the service IGs have the same basic investigative process as outlined above, each service has adapted process specifics to its own circumstances. Each service reviews and approves the investigations it conducts at the service's headquarter IG before forwarding them to DODIG for final approval. Table 2 outlines differences among the services and DODIG in how they investigate reprisal cases.

Table 2: Reprisal Process Implementation Differences by Investigating Organization

	DODIG	Army[a]	Navy[a]	Marine Corps[a]	Air Force[a]
Level at which the investigation is conducted	DODIG conducts investigations and provides oversight and approval of all Service IG cases	Organization-level and above[b] with Army IG headquarters (HQ) oversight	Echelon II[c] Command level, with Navy IG HQ oversight	Marine Corps IG HQ	Wing level and above with Air Force IG HQ oversight
Number of legal reviews required for full investigations[d]	1 conducted at DODIG	1 required at the level where case is investigated	2; 1 conducted at Echelon II Command level and 1 required at Navy IG HQ	1 required at Marine Corps IG HQ level	2; 1 conducted at Major Command and 1 required at Air Force IG HQ
Investigator status	Primarily civilian	Primarily military	Primarily civilian	Civilian only	Mix depending on the level at which investigated
Mean number of cases closed per year by investigating organization[e]	66[f]	158	41	4	135
Active and reserve military servicemember population[g]	—	1,132,600	394,200	241,700	510,100

Source: GAO analysis of DOD information.

[a]The services investigate cases for both their active and reserve components.

[b]Army organizations—which are generally at the division level—have IGs assigned to them. These IGs are similar to installation-level IGs.

[c]Echelon II Commands have senior level of authority and report directly to the Chief of Naval Operations (CNO) and would be the equivalent of a major command.

[d]Based on requirements articulated by officials from the organizations noted. Additionally, both Navy and Marine Corps also require a legal sufficiency review for cases that do not go to full investigation.

[e]Mean number of cases closed per year by investigating organization based on data for all military whistleblower reprisal cases closed between fiscal year 2006 and the first half of fiscal year 2011 (October 1, 2005 through March 31, 2011).

[f]In addition to having conducted a mean of 66 investigations per year during this time period, DODIG also provided oversight reviews for the investigations completed by the service IGs.

[g]Active and reserve military servicemember population figures are the fiscal year 2011 estimates in DOD's Defense Manpower Requirements Report: Fiscal Year 2011 (December 2010).

Appendix II provides more information on the characteristics of military whistleblower reprisal cases.

DODIG Is Generally Not Meeting Timeliness Requirements and Improvement Efforts Are Hindered by Unreliable and Incomplete Data

DODIG has taken multiple steps, in collaboration with the service IGs in some instances, to improve DOD's ability to process military whistleblower reprisal cases in a timely manner. However, DOD has generally not met statutory requirements to provide reports on completed investigations within 180 days of the date the allegation was made or alternatively, to provide notice to the complainant and the Secretary of Defense. The July 2009 Department of Justice IG report found that lingering investigations leave complainants without resolution to their concern and could hold up a potential promotion for a subject. In addition, DODIG's May 2011 review of its military whistleblower reprisal process raised concerns that some complainants withdrew their cases because of the length of time it takes to complete investigations.[23] Further, DOD's efforts to improve processing time have been hindered by unreliable and incomplete data. Moreover, DODIG does not report data on timeliness in its semiannual reports, thereby limiting the information Congress could use to provide oversight of the military whistleblower reprisal program.

DODIG Faces Challenges in the Timely Processing of Reprisal Cases

DODIG and the service IGs have faced challenges to processing military whistleblower reprisal cases in a timely manner which they attribute to staffing shortages and process inefficiencies. Although DODIG has taken multiple steps, in collaboration with the service IGs in some instances, to improve processing time, these efforts have not yet resulted in meeting the statutory requirement to provide reports on completed investigations within 180 days of the date the allegation was made.[24] Timeliness is a key challenge and an important factor in completing quality investigations because, without timely resolutions, the reliability of evidence could suffer, and the careers of both the complainants and subjects could be negatively impacted.

---

[23] U.S. Department of Defense Inspector General, *"Review of the Office of Deputy Inspector General for Administrative Investigations, Directorate for Military Reprisal Investigations,"* May 2011.

[24] Under 10 U.S.C. §1034 (e)(3), the IG investigating a military whistleblower reprisal investigation must complete an investigation report within 180 days. If the investigating IG determines it is not possible to complete the report within 180 days of the date the allegation under investigation was made, the IG must notify the complainant and the Secretary of Defense that this deadline cannot be met and of the reasons why, as well as a time when the report will be completed.

DOD Directive 7050.06 addresses the need to conduct investigations expeditiously.[25] Officials at DODIG and the service IGs stated that staffing levels are a key factor in determining the timely processing of reprisal cases. According to DODIG, the military whistleblower reprisal caseload has grown significantly since the enactment of the Military Whistleblower Protection Act, and staffing has not kept up with the increased caseload. Further, service IG officials told us that DODIG's review of service investigations can be slow because of understaffing. DODIG has taken action on this issue, increasing the staffing of its whistleblower reprisal directorate from 17 staff in fiscal year 2006 to 30 staff in fiscal year 2011 to accommodate the increased caseload. In January 2012, DOD's Acting Inspector General authorized a further increase of staff for its whistleblower reprisal directorate from 30 to 42 (see fig. 3 for staffing at DODIG from fiscal years 2006 through 2011). Some service IG officials also indicated that staffing shortages are a factor in their ability to process cases in a timely manner. In a December 2011 letter, the DOD Inspector General asked the secretaries of the military departments to consider favorably any requests from the service IGs to increase their staffing in order to deal with the increased number of whistleblower reprisal cases.

[25] DOD Directive 7050.06, *Military Whistleblower Protection* (July 23, 2007).

Figure 3: Average Number of Staff at the DODIG Military Whistleblower Reprisal Directorate from Fiscal Year 2006 through Fiscal Year 2011

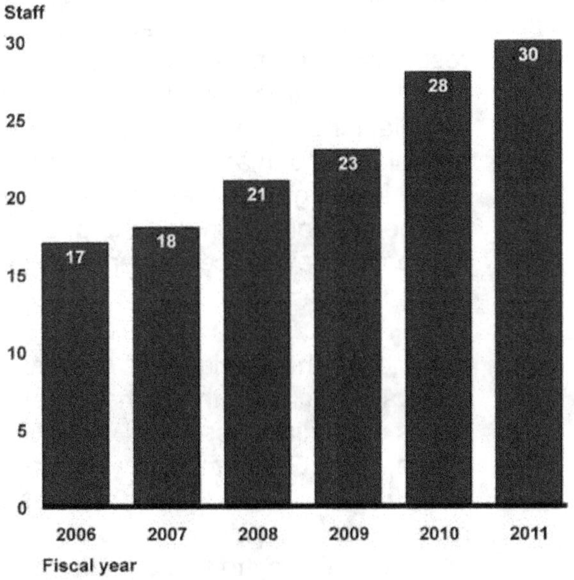

Staff

Fiscal year	Staff
2006	17
2007	18
2008	21
2009	23
2010	28
2011	30

Fiscal year

Source: GAO analysis of DODIG data.

Note: According to DODIG officials, the directorate responsible for investigating military whistleblower reprisals also had two detailees assigned to it in fiscal year 2009.

DODIG has also undertaken multiple efforts to reform its investigative process to improve timeliness. For example, in late 2010, DODIG eliminated an investigative phase which required formal reports that recommended whether or not a case should be fully investigated. Earlier that year, DODIG eliminated the committee charged with reviewing and approving whether cases should be fully investigated. DODIG also changed its process for taking in complaints. The Defense Hotline[26] used to document the original complaint, gather additional information from complainants, and send it to the directorate at DODIG responsible for

---

[26] The Defense Hotline is a DODIG program responsible for taking in all types of complaints for DOD in addition to whistleblower reprisal complaints. Its activities are governed by Department of Defense Instruction 7050.01, *Defense Hotline Program* (Dec. 17, 2007). The Defense Hotline receives and investigates complaints or information concerning allegations of violations of law, rules or regulations, mismanagement, gross waste of funds, abuse of authority, and a substantial and specific threat to the public health and safety involving the Department of Defense.

military whistleblower reprisal investigations. The Defense Hotline also was responsible for communicating with complainants if their cases were determined not to be whistleblower reprisal cases. Now the Defense Hotline passes the reprisal allegation to the directorate at DODIG responsible for military whistleblower reprisal investigations and investigators from that directorate establish direct contact with the complainant to assess the validity of the reprisal allegation(s). DODIG officials stated this new intake process is faster and increases the quality of the investigations because experienced reprisal investigators are in charge of information gathering. DODIG also started testing a new approach in evidence gathering to determine whether it can close cases more quickly.[27]

In contrast, the service IGs' processes for investigating these cases have generally remained the same. One major exception is the way Army cases are initially assessed. In order to deal with a large backlog in Army cases, DODIG and the Army IG signed a Memorandum of Agreement in 2008 whereby DODIG took over responsibility for conducting the initial review of all incoming Army complaints. The Memorandum of Agreement allowed the Army to focus on investigations and thereby reduce the Army's backlog of cases. Army and DODIG officials stated that this agreement was successful in reducing the Army's case backlog and improving case processing time.[28] Yet DODIG formally notified the Army IG in November 2011 that it would terminate this special arrangement as of May 2012. DODIG officials told us that they did so in order to maintain a consistent approach among the services and because the arrangement had increased DODIG's workload. In addition, they told us that cancelling the arrangement would enable their staff to conduct more full investigations. In November 2011, the Army IG asked DODIG to reconsider this decision, stating that the timeliness of Army reprisal

---

[27] The new approach is a beta-test where DODIG allows its investigators to speak with subjects at the onset of an inquiry or initial analysis to determine if the case warrants full investigation. The previous process did not allow investigators to speak with subjects unless the case definitely went to full investigation.

[28] The 2009 Department of Justice IG report recommended that DODIG consider whether it should take responsibility for conducting the initial review for the incoming complaints from all of the services, not just those from the Army. In its October 2011 action plan, DODIG stated it would assess how well the service IGs are performing intake of reprisal complaints in late fiscal year 2012 and that DODIG would evaluate the Department of Justice IG recommendation that DODIG consider conducting initial reviews of all service reprisal complaints after it has implemented some of its other reforms.

investigations would suffer.[29] However, in December 2011, DODIG affirmed its decision to end the agreement with the Army.

Although DODIG has undertaken these and other efforts to improve its timeliness, it has generally not been completing investigations within the 180-day time frame provided by law. From our analysis of a random sample of 91 cases closed between January 1, 2009 through March 31, 2011, we estimate that 70 percent of the cases were not completed within 180 days; moreover, we estimated that it took DOD a mean of 451 days (+/- 94 days) to process the cases. Our random sample included a subset of 61 inquiries closed before full investigation, which took a mean of 469 days to close, and a subset of 28 full investigations, which took a mean of 395 days to close.[30,31] See table 3 for case processing time according to investigative phase.

---

[29] The Army IG also expressed concerns that process reforms made by DODIG since early 2011 had reversed gains the Army IG was beginning to see in the processing of military whistleblower reprisal complaints.

[30] Although case processing time for the full sample is generalizable, it is not generalizable for any subset. Additionally, the case processing time data reported for the two investigative phase subsets are based on 89 of the 91 cases we analyzed. For the investigative phase subsets, we excluded 2 additional cases because we could not identify the investigative phase in which they were closed based on the evidence in the case file.

[31] For the subset of inquiries closed before full investigation, the median days to close a case was 249, with a range from 14 to 2,215 days. For full investigations, the median days to close a case was 349, with a range from 51 to 1,181 days.

Table 3: Mean Case Processing Time by Investigative Phase of Sampled Cases Closed between January 1, 2009 and March 31, 2011

Investigative phase	Number assessed	Total days (mean)	Percentage of cases over 180 days
All cases	91	451 (+/- 94 days)	70% (+/- 11%)
Cases closed before full investigation	61	469	64% (39 of 61 cases)
Full investigation	28	395	82% (23 of 28 cases)

☐ Data generalizable

☐ Data not generalizable

Source: GAO review of military whistleblower reprisal case files maintained by DODIG.

Notes:

Our random sample of 91 cases (out of a total of 871 cases closed during this time period) included 61 inquiries closed before full investigation and 28 cases closed after a full investigation. We were unable to determine the investigative phase in which 2 cases were closed.

Although data from the full sample are representative within the given parameters, any subset of these data cannot be assumed to be representative. That is, data specific to the cases closed before full investigation and the data specific to full investigation are not generalizable and apply only to the actual cases reviewed.

In addition to not completing investigations in 180 days in most cases, DOD has not complied with the statutory reporting requirement to provide notification in those instances where the investigations go beyond 180 days, although it is taking steps to do so.[32] The Military Whistleblower Protection Act requires the IG investigating an allegation of reprisal to submit to the Secretary of Defense and the complainant a notice if it cannot provide a report on the completed investigation within 180 days of

---

[32] 10 U.S.C. §1034 (e)(3) requires the IG investigating the allegation of reprisal to submit to the Secretary of Defense and the complainant a notice if they determine it is not possible to submit an investigative report within 180 days after receiving the allegation. The notice to the Secretary of Defense and the complainant is to contain a determination that the report may not be submitted on time and the reasons for the delay, as well as the time when the report will be submitted. DOD Directive 7050.06 assigns responsibility for providing these reports to DODIG. The directive also directs the service IGs to submit reports of investigation to DODIG within 180 days and if unable to do so, directs them to provide notice to the DODIG in addition to the complainant and the office designated to receive notice on behalf of the Secretary of Defense. The directive requires DOD component IGs other than the service IGs to provide DODIG with a report of investigation within 180 days from the date DODIG requested an investigation, but does not require them to provide notice if the 180 day time frame is exceeded.

the date the allegation was made to an IG in DOD. The notice should include the reason for the delay and an expected completion date for the investigation.[33] DODIG officials acknowledged that they and the services had not been making the required notifications. The officials stated they used to submit these reports to the Secretary of Defense, but stopped doing so at some point because they were told by officials at the office receiving the notifications that they did not know what to do with the information.[34] Because this notification is not being provided, as required by statute, the Secretary of Defense has had reduced visibility of cases that exceed the investigative time limit, and complainants have not been receiving information regarding their cases to which the law entitles them. During the course of our review, DODIG changed its practice and started reporting this information in October 2011. According to its October 2011 action plan, DODIG is taking steps to ensure that it and the service IGs follow the statutory reporting requirements.

DOD Efforts to Improve Case Processing Times Have Been Hindered by Unreliable and Incomplete Data

Although DOD has taken some steps to improve the timeliness of investigations, its efforts are hampered because DODIG does not have key timeliness data that would allow it to identify process areas requiring improvement or evaluate the impact of reforms. According to the quality standards for investigations, developed by the Council of the Inspectors General on Integrity and Efficiency, organizations should store data in a manner that allows for effective retrieval, referencing, and analysis. This enhances an organization's ability to conduct pattern and trend analyses and assists in the process of making informed judgments on investigative program development, and in the implementation of the investigative

---

[33] DOD Directive 7050.06 requires the investigating organization to submit notice to the complainant as well as to the Deputy Under Secretary of Defense for Program Integration within the Office of the Secretary of Defense. Responsibility for receiving notices was shifted to the Office of the Under Secretary of Defense for Personnel and Readiness—Enterprise Services in December 2011 (see table 1 on roles and responsibilities).

[34] DODIG officials could not recall when they stopped sending the notifications to the Secretary of Defense for investigations that were not closed within 180 days of the date the allegation was made. Officials from the office currently responsible for receiving these notifications (Office of the Under Secretary of Defense for Personnel and Readiness—Enterprise Services) had no record of receiving such notifications. Further, our case file review of 91 cases closed between January 1, 2009 and March 31, 2011, included 64 cases that were not closed within 180 days. We did not find evidence in any of these 64 case files that the Secretary of Defense had been notified. However, we did find evidence in 2 of the 64 cases of notifications sent to complainants.

process.[35] Further, our prior work has shown that tracking timeliness is important for accountability and for making improvements to investigative processes.[36]

In our assessment of its data, we found that DODIG has not consistently or accurately recorded key dates to track how long investigations take to complete. From our analysis of a random sample of cases closed between January 1, 2009 through March 31, 2011, we estimate that DODIG's database understated the amount of days it took to close cases by a mean of 193 days (+/-76 days).[37] The understated number of days was a result of DODIG officials recording the date that they received a complaint in their office rather than the original date the complainant made the allegation to an IG in DOD. In addition, our case file review found that DODIG identified three cases as closed in its database when it actually referred these cases to a service for further investigation, resulting in an understatement of the amount of time it took to close cases. In one of these three cases, it took an additional 872 days to close the case. Moreover, our case file review found that 7 full investigations out of 28 had correct dates recorded in DODIG's database.[38] Table 4 provides timeliness accuracy by investigative phase.

---

[35] Council of the Inspectors General on Integrity and Efficiency, *Quality Standards for Investigations* (Nov. 15, 2011). The Council of the Inspectors General on Integrity and Efficiency gets its authority from Section 11 of the Inspector General Act of 1978 (5 U.S.C. app. 3.), as amended. The mission of the Council of the Inspectors General on Integrity and Efficiency shall be to address integrity, economy, and effectiveness issues that transcend individual government agencies and increase the professionalism and effectiveness of personnel by developing policies, standards, and approaches to aid in the establishment of a well-trained and highly skilled workforce in the Offices of Inspectors General.

[36] GAO, *Personnel Security Clearances: Progress Has Been Made to Improve Timeliness but Continued Oversight Is Needed to Sustain Momentum*, GAO-11-65 (Washington, D.C.: Nov. 19, 2010).

[37] From our analysis of a random sample of cases closed between January 1, 2009 through March 31, 2011, we estimate that DODIG accurately recorded the case received dates 30 percent of the time and accurately recorded the case closed dates 93 percent of the time.

[38] We considered cases to have accurate dates if the dates in the database and supporting documentation in the actual case file matched for both the received and closed dates.

Table 4: Timeliness Accuracy by Investigative Phase of Sampled Cases Closed between January 1, 2009 and March 31, 2011

Case type	Number assessed	Mean amount of days (DODIG database)	Actual mean amount of days (case file review)	Cases with accurately recorded dates in DODIG database
All cases	91	258 *(+/- 93 days)*	451 *(+/- 94 days)*	33% *(+/- 11%)*
Cases closed before full investigation	61	271	469	38% *(23 of 61 cases)*
Full investigation	28	242	395	25% *(7 of 28 cases)*

☐ Data generalizable

☐ Data not generalizable

Source: GAO review of military whistleblower reprisal case files maintained by DODIG.

Notes:

Our random sample of 91 cases (out of a total of 871 cases closed during this time period) included 61 inquiries closed before full investigation and 28 cases closed after a full investigation. We were unable to determine the investigative phase in which 2 cases were closed.

Although data from the full sample are representative within the given parameters, any subset of these data cannot be assumed to be representative. That is, data specific to the cases closed before full investigation and the data specific to full investigation are not generalizable and apply only to the actual cases reviewed.

DODIG's data practices have inhibited its ability to accurately identify the age of cases and therefore also prevented it from identifying cases in danger of exceeding the 180 days provided for investigations by the Military Whistleblower Protection Act. DODIG has acknowledged it has problems with data reliability, calling the integrity of its data "questionable at best" in its October 2011 action plan for reforming the military whistleblower reprisal program. Further, during the course of our review, DODIG officials acknowledged that some of their dates for tracking cases were inaccurate. DODIG changed its approach starting in fiscal year 2012 so it now accurately records total case processing time. DODIG officials said they also planned to train investigators to ensure they consistently enter this information into DODIG's database.

In addition, DODIG has not been tracking the time the separate phases of the investigative process take. We found that the DODIG database includes fields for tracking dates by phases in the process. For example, there are date fields for referring cases to services for investigation and date fields for receiving those investigations from the services, but these were generally not filled out. Further, DODIG was not tracking the amount of time between when a complaint was filed with the Defense Hotline to when it was assigned to an investigator. We have previously found that comprehensive information is needed to identify reasons for delays in investigative processes.[39] DODIG officials acknowledged they can track timeliness data by process phases using their current systems and that doing so would enable them to understand the entire life cycle of military whistleblower reprisal investigations. Without identifying, collecting, and tracking accurate data, DODIG does not have reliable information to identify the scope of the challenge it faces with overall timeliness and cannot report accurate data to internal and external stakeholders, including data it reports in its semiannual reports to Congress. Moreover, DODIG may be unable to identify possible areas in the investigative process needing improvement, or assess the impact on timeliness of recent changes made to its process or of other actions taken to improve timeliness. During the course of our review, DODIG developed a plan to improve its practices associated with collecting and tracking timeliness information, including identifying date fields it should track, and training investigators to consistently enter this information. DODIG began to initiate these improvements starting in fiscal year 2012.

Congressional oversight of DODIG's ongoing efforts to improve data collection and management is hindered by the lack of available timeliness data. According to the *Standards for Internal Control in the Federal Government*, managers should provide reliable, useful, and timely information for accountability of government programs and their operations.[40] Although oversight is important for accountability, the IGs are intended to be independent and objective units, according to the Inspector General Act of 1978. Under the act, DODIG is not subject to regular organizational oversight inside DOD.[41] As a result, the Office of the Under Secretary of Defense for Personnel and Readiness—the organization designated by directive to receive notifications regarding reprisal investigations that exceed the 180-day time period, on behalf of

---

[39] GAO, *DOD Personnel Clearances: Comprehensive Timeliness Reporting, Complete Clearance Documentation, and Quality Measures Are Needed to Further Improve the Clearance Process*, GAO-09-400 (Washington, D.C.: May 19, 2009).

[40] GAO, *Standards for Internal Control in the Federal Government*, GAO/AIMD-00-21.3.1 (Washington, D.C.: Nov. 1, 1999).

[41] According to section 3 of appendix 3 of Title 5 of the United States Code, each Inspector General shall report to and be under the general supervision of the head of the establishment involved or, to the extent such authority is delegated, the officer next in rank below such head, but shall not report to, or be subject to supervision by, any other officer of such establishment.

the Secretary of Defense[42]—cannot provide organizational oversight of DODIG.[43] DODIG officials stated that, although other offices within DOD cannot provide this type of oversight, the reporting requirement acts as a helpful internal check for DODIG on its timeliness progress. Congress is therefore the primary oversight body for DODIG. DODIG is required to keep Congress fully and currently informed through, among other things, its semiannual reports to Congress. That report is required to include information on fraud, abuses, and deficiencies relating to the administration of programs and operations managed or financed by DOD.[44] DODIG has not previously interpreted this requirement as applying to the military whistleblower reprisal program and does not provide information on military whistleblower reprisal case processing time, including the proportion of cases that exceed the 180-day time period provided by law, in the semiannual reports. However, the absence of timeliness information in these reports limits congressional decision makers' ability to thoroughly evaluate and identify whether delays continue to exist within DOD's whistleblower reprisal investigative process. As a result, Congress lacks information it could use to provide oversight of the military whistleblower reprisal program.

---

[42] DOD Directive 7050.06 (July 23, 2007).

[43] Department of Defense Directive 5106.01, *Inspector General of the Department of Defense* (Apr. 13, 2006), establishes that the Inspector General of the Department of Defense shall report to and be under the general supervision of the Secretary of Defense and the Deputy Secretary of Defense, but shall not report to, or be subject to supervision by, any other officer of the Department of Defense. The directive also states that neither the Secretary of Defense nor the Deputy Secretary of Defense shall prevent or prohibit the Inspector General of the Department of Defense from initiating, carrying out, or completing any audit, evaluation, inspection, or investigation, unless otherwise specified in law.

[44] See 5 U.S.C. App. 3, §5 and Department of Defense Directive 5106.01, par. 5.17 (Apr. 13, 2006).

DODIG Is Taking Steps to Address Whistleblower Reprisal Process Weaknesses but Oversight Challenges Remain

In an effort to improve its whistleblower program, DODIG has taken steps such as responding to the 2009 Department of Justice IG recommendations, completing an internal review, restructuring the organization primarily responsible for providing program oversight, and developing a plan of action. However, DODIG's oversight of this program still faces challenges because of the lack of performance metrics, outdated and inconsistently followed guidance, and the lack of standard monitoring processes and procedures for investigative cases.

DODIG Is Taking Steps to Address External and Internal Recommended Actions

DODIG has taken steps to improve the whistleblower reprisal process, including acting on prior recommendations. The 2009 Department of Justice report highlighted weaknesses in the military whistleblower program and made recommendations for improvements such as creating and updating written policy guidance regarding whistleblower law.[45] DODIG conducted an internal review, completed in 2011, to assess the progress it had made since beginning to take actions to address the findings of the Department of Justice report.[46] This report made additional recommendations to help improve DODIG's oversight of the whistleblower reprisal program, including that DODIG conduct an internal audit of its case tracking system to help ensure timely case processing.

In October 2011, DODIG developed an action plan that outlined its strategy to address the program weaknesses identified in the 2009 Department of Justice report and its 2011 internal review, and has begun to implement that strategy. We have already mentioned some of the changes DODIG is undertaking based on the action plan, including changes to the report review processes. As part of the reform plan, DODIG restructured its directorate in charge of military whistleblower reprisal investigations in October 2011, merging it with the directorate responsible for civilian whistleblower reprisal investigations. One of the goals of this merger is to increase the consistency of reprisal

---

[45] U.S. Department of Justice, *A Review of the Department of Defense Office of Inspector General's Process for Handling Military Whistleblower Reprisal Allegations* (July 2009).

[46] U.S. Department of Defense Inspector General, *Review of Office of Deputy Inspector General for Administrative Investigations, Directorate for Military Reprisal Investigations* (May 2011).

investigations within DOD. Additionally, the merger is intended to eventually create a pool of investigators that can work on both military and civilian reprisal cases, thereby maximizing DODIG's flexibility to adjust to spikes in reprisal cases and clear any case backlogs. The immediate past DOD Inspector General also told us that one of the most significant changes he made was putting a robust new leadership team in place dedicated to improving the military whistleblower reprisal program and transforming it into a model program.

DODIG has also revised its case intake process as part of its reform efforts. Reprisal allegations that are made directly to DODIG rather than a service can come in through the Defense Hotline over the phone or using an automated web-based form. DODIG has made multiple changes in the last several years to its process for taking in and initially assessing if these cases qualify as reprisal cases. The 2011 internal review found that DODIG's intake process was still requiring complainants to provide a significant amount of documentary evidence to support their reprisal allegations. The internal review concluded the emphasis on documentation at this very early stage just to determine if the allegations warranted investigation was inconsistent with the basic information required when filing complaints with the Defense Hotline. Further, the internal review found that the documentation demands required at this stage could produce an onerous burden for the complainant and were inconsistent with DODIG guidance. In response, DODIG is instituting changes to quickly assign an investigator to a case, who then makes direct contact with the complainant and initiates an investigation based on the standard that, "the alleged fact, if true, would raise the inference of reprisal."

DOD's Implementation of Oversight Mechanisms Is Not Yet Complete and Faces Challenges

Although DODIG has taken steps to improve its military whistleblower reprisal program, its ability to provide oversight continues to face key challenges due to the lack of performance metrics, outdated and inconsistently followed guidance, and inconsistent monitoring processes and procedures to track all reprisal allegations. According to Standards for Internal Control in the Federal Government, oversight mechanisms are an integral part of an entity's planning, implementing, reviewing, and of the accountability for stewardship of government resources and achieving effective results.[47] Oversight mechanisms include, among other things, the written policies, procedures, techniques, performance measures, and mechanisms that enforce management's directives and help ensure that actions can be taken to address risks. While DOD's action plan offers many important steps towards achieving a model whistleblower reprisal program, these actions are ongoing, and to date have not been fully implemented.

Performance Metrics

DODIG has not yet fully established performance metrics for whistleblower investigations although it is taking steps to do so. Federal internal control standards say metrics are important for identifying and setting appropriate incentives for achieving goals while complying with law, regulations, and ethical standards.[48] DODIG officials recognize the importance of metrics and have told us that they are currently working to create timeliness metrics that focus on case processing time. However, they have not yet formalized these metrics. We have previously found that timeliness alone does not provide a complete picture of an investigative process and that metrics on quality, such as completeness of investigative reports and the adequacy of internal controls, enhance the ability of organizations to provide assurance that it is exercising all of the appropriate safeguards for federal programs.[49] Further, measuring timeliness alone may provide incentive to close cases prematurely.[50] For example, DODIG could theoretically close and report on all cases before they reach 180 days in order to meet the timeliness standard. However, meeting that standard alone would not ensure that cases were properly investigated. DODIG currently lacks metrics to measure quality, but DODIG officials recognize that metrics on quality are important and indicated that they plan to develop them as part of their effort to improve case management and outcomes. The officials said that such metrics could include measuring whether interviews are completed and

---

[47] GAO, *Standards for Internal Control in the Federal Government*, GAO/AIMD-00-21.3.1 (Washington, D.C.: Nov. 1, 1999).

[48] GAO, *Internal Control Management and Evaluation Tool,* GAO-01-1008G (Washington, D.C.: Aug. 2001).

[49] GAO, *DOD Personnel Clearances: Comprehensive Timeliness Reporting, Complete Clearance Documentation, and Quality Measures Are Needed to Further Improve the Clearance Process*, GAO-09-400 (Washington, D.C.: May 19, 2009).

[50] GAO, *Whistleblower Protection: Sustained Management Attention Needed to Address Long-standing Program Weaknesses*, GAO-10-722 (Washington, D.C.: Aug.17, 2010).

documented and whether conclusions made about the case are fully supported by evidence.

Our review of case files revealed that documents that could be used to support the conclusions of a case were not always present in DODIG's case files. For example, according to DODIG's investigations manual,[51] every case file should have some sort of documented investigative analysis that lays out the evidence and conclusions the evidence supports. The level of investigative analysis we looked for in each case file depended on how far the case proceeded. For cases that were closed in the very early stages of the investigation, an oversight worksheet summarizing the reasons for closing a case was sufficient for the purpose of our file review. For cases that went to full investigation, we looked for a formal record of investigation. We found evidence of investigative analysis in 79 (87 percent) of the 91 case files. Additionally, DODIG requires that investigations that go beyond the initial review include a record of testimony from the complainant. Full investigations are also required to include a record of an interview with the subject. When reviewing the cases for this document, we found evidence of a record of testimony in 38 (49 percent) of the 77 cases that required it. Although we looked in our case file review for the types of documents that would support DODIG's conclusions, we did not determine whether the evidence in each file actually supported DODIG's conclusions for each case. However, an internal DODIG review found that some cases DODIG adjudicated contained insufficient documentation to support the findings or evidence that necessary investigative steps were completed. The internal review team further noted that they did not disagree with the final outcomes of the cases, only that they could not affirm the decisions because the information in some of the file did not support it. Without clear quality metrics, DODIG will continue to lack valuable information it could use to improve oversight of the whistleblower reprisal investigative process.

Guidance

Although DODIG is updating its outdated guidance related to the whistleblower program, the updates have not yet been formalized and the existing guidance is inconsistently followed. According to the framework set out in quality standards for investigations, organizations should

---

[51] DOD Inspector General Office of the Deputy Inspector General for Investigations, *Investigations Manual Reprisal and Senior Official Cases* (Mar. 2006).

establish appropriate written investigative policies and procedures through handbook, manual, directives, or similar mechanism to facilitate due professional care in meeting program requirements.[52] Further, that guidance should be regularly evaluated to ensure that it is still appropriate and working as intended. DODIG has guidance regarding the whistleblower reprisal process in place but has not updated it to reflect changes in its investigative practices or ensured that certain provisions have been carried out consistently. For example, DODIG's primary investigative guide distributed to investigators conducting whistleblower reprisal investigations has not been updated since 1996 and does not reflect some current investigative practices.[53] The investigative guide directs investigators to appendices that no longer exist and states that whistleblower reprisal investigation reports must be completed and issued within 90 days of the receipt of the allegation instead of the 180 days provided under the statute as amended in 1998. Officials from the service IGs told us that the old guidance still provides them with some benefit regarding general investigative approaches but said that it would be beneficial to them if it was updated. Additionally, DODIG officials acknowledge that the current guidance reflects old investigative approaches that have since been revised, such as the investigator checklist, or that no longer exist. The lack of updated guidance has been a recurring issue for DODIG. A 2002 DODIG briefing stated that the investigative guide required updating and that the update was nearing completion. The 2009 Department of Justice IG report also found that guidance for service IGs had not been adequate and that DODIG could improve oversight of service IG work by creating and updating written policy guidance regarding whistleblower law, including recurring and emerging issues, best practices, and precedent. Moreover, the 2011 internal review came to a similar conclusion and recommended that DODIG update the investigative guides to ensure consistency and objectivity in processing cases. DODIG indicated that it planned to revise its investigative guidance in both its response to the Department of Justice report as well as in its response to the 2011 internal review. DODIG officials told us that they are working with internal stakeholders to revise the guidance to reflect current practices and plan on updating the

---

[52] Council of the Inspectors General on Integrity and Efficiency, *Quality Standards for Investigations* (Nov. 15, 2011).

[53] DOD Inspector General Departmental Guidance 7050.6, *Guide to Investigating Reprisal and Improper Referrals for Mental Health Evaluations* (Feb. 6, 1996).

1996 investigative by the third quarter of fiscal year 2012. Without updated guidance on investigations, DODIG does not have a documented consistent investigative standard for its whistleblower program.

In addition to being outdated, DODIG's existing guidance related to the whistleblower program is not consistently followed. We have reported that program guidance should be regularly evaluated to ensure that it is still appropriate and working as intended.[54] The guidance related to certain key provisions of the investigative process is unclear, leading to inconsistent implementation among the service IGs. For example, the service IGs have adopted different interpretations of the 180-day reporting requirement as it is set out in the guidance. As noted earlier in the report, the Military Whistleblower Protection Act requires that IGs conducting investigations issue a report of investigation to the complainant and the Secretary of Defense within 180 days of the receipt of an allegation or provide appropriate notice if unable to do so. The law also requires DODIG to approve the report of investigation before the report is issued. Further, officials from DODIG and the service IGs emphasized that whistleblower reprisal cases are not closed until DODIG has reviewed the complaint and the evidence to support the investigators' conclusions and formally agrees with the disposition of the case. However, DOD Directive 7050.06 sets out additional time frames for reporting. The directive requires the service IGs to provide DODIG with a report of investigation within 180 days of receiving the complaint or receiving a request for an investigation from DODIG and requires them to provide a report of investigation to the complainant and the Secretary of Defense not later than 30 days after the DODIG approves the report. A service IG could meet the first requirement but at the same time leave no time for DODIG to review and approve the report in time to issue it within the 180 days provided by law.[55] As a result, the service IGs have adopted different interpretations of the directive's 180-day reporting requirement. For example, Air Force IG officials told us that the Air Force recently reinterpreted the reporting requirement. The Air Force had set an internal goal of completing reprisal investigation within 135 days to allow 45 days for DODIG review and approval. However, the Air Force told us that it

---

[54] GAO-01-1008G.

[55] As noted previously, the Military Whistleblower Protection Act and DOD Directive 7050.06 both allow alternative notification to the Secretary of Defense and the complainant if the 180 days provided by law are going to be exceeded.

now sets its internal investigation deadline to 180 days and therefore no longer accounts for DODIG review time. The Army IG stated that it had the same interpretation of the 180-day reporting requirement as the Air Force IG. Officials from the Navy and Marine Corps IGs told us they generally include DODIG review in their interpretation of the 180-day reporting requirement. DODIG officials are aware of some of the different interpretations among the services and the conflicts that exist in the current directive. According to DODIG, it will be sending written guidance to the services to reemphasize that the 180-day statutory time frame is prescribed as from the time the complaint is filed until the time the report is submitted to the complainant. DODIG reported that it will also incorporate the clarifying language into the directive and will begin the process of revising DOD Directive 7050.06 in the second quarter of 2012.

DODIG also has not been consistently adhering to standards regarding the maintenance of its case files and, as a result, its case files are generally incomplete. Quality Standards for Investigations outline standards related to case file management and state that the file folders used to document an investigation should be accurate and complete, and the investigative report findings and accomplishments must be supported by adequate documentation and maintained in the case file.[56] According to DODIG's standards related to the management of these files, it is important for case files to adequately represent the investigative work and evidence underlying the conclusions and recommendations in the final report, and to be thoroughly documented to ensure that the files will be able to withstand scrutiny.[57] Based on a review of DODIG's process, relevant statutes, directives, and other standards, and in consultation with DODIG officials, we identified 18 key elements that we believe should be present in case files to provide support for conclusions, document compliance with the law or directives, or help manage the case. Using our sample of 91 cases, we assessed the presence of the key elements as indicators of the completeness of the file.[58] Based on the presence in the

---

[56] Council of the Inspectors General on Integrity and Efficiency, *Quality Standards for Investigations* (Nov. 15, 2011).

[57] DOD Inspector General Office of the Deputy Inspector General for Investigations, *Investigations Manual Reprisal and Senior Official Cases* (March 2006).

[58] Some of these elements included specific documents. For example, the Army oversight worksheet was a specific document. Other elements could be reflected in multiple documents. For example, the sequence of key events could be in a larger report, be in a summary, or be its own document. For further details on our methodology, see app. I.

file of the elements we selected, we found that most of DODIG's case files were incomplete (56 percent) or partially complete (38 percent) and only a small portion of the case files were complete (5 percent). See table 5 for further details.

Table 5: Estimated Level of DODIG Case File Folder Completeness for Cases Closed between January 1, 2009 and March 31, 2011

Level of case file completeness	Number of cases (out of 91)	Percentage of cases
Complete[a]	5	5% (+/-11%)
Partially complete[b]	35	38% (+/-11%)
Incomplete[c]	51	56% (+/-11%)

Source: GAO analysis of DOD information.

Notes:

Based on a review of 91 files of the original random sample of 97 for cases closed between January 1, 2009 and March 31, 2011.

Percentages do not add up to 100 percent due to rounding.

We identified 18 elements and used those as indicators for the completeness of a file. However, not all 18 elements needed to be present in every file. For example, some of the 18 elements would only need to be present in a file if an investigation was conducted by a service, went beyond 180 days, or was a full investigation. We adjusted the required number of elements based on the specific circumstances of each case and calculated completeness based on that adjusted baseline. See app. I for further details on the scope and methodology.

[a]We assessed a case file to be complete if it contained 85 percent or more of the documents that should be present.

[b]We assessed a case file to be partially complete if it contained between 70 and 84 percent of the documents that should be present.

[c]We assessed a case file to be incomplete if it contained less than 70 percent of the documents that should be present.

We also found that the guidance regarding a key investigative question is unclear. According to DODIG's investigative guide,[59] an investigation is complete when the four questions of the "Acid Test" have been answered (see fig. 2). We estimate that 65 percent of the cases closed between January 1, 2009 and March 31, 2011, were closed, at least in part, because DODIG concluded that the personnel action would have occurred even if the protected communication had not been made—question 4 of the Acid Test (see app. II for further details on the reasons

---

[59] DOD Inspector General Departmental Guidance 7050.6, *Guide to Investigating Reprisal and Improper Referrals for Mental Health Evaluations* (Feb. 6, 1996).

GAO-12-362 Whistleblower Protection

DODIG closed cases). The departmental guidance for addressing all four questions instructs the investigator to investigate the complaint, and not the complainant, noting that investigators should avoid the tendency to examine the reputation, background, or performance of the complainant in order to determine the credibility of the complainant's claim. However, in answering the fourth question, the guidance requires, among other things, an examination of the reasonableness of the unfavorable personnel action(s) taken, withheld, or threatened considering the complainant's performance and conduct. DODIG officials acknowledged that there may be some tension between these two requirements. Further, in its October 2011 action plan, DODIG stated that current guidance for question 4 has resulted in investigators closing cases prematurely without fully considering whether the subject's actions are consistent with actions taken in similar situations with other employees. As a result, DODIG officials are revising guidance for the investigative questions. However, until DODIG carries out these actions, the lack of clear guidance hinders efforts to ensure consistent program implementation.

Case Monitoring Processes and Procedures

DODIG officials acknowledge the importance of standard case monitoring processes and procedures, but currently lack such processes and procedures, which may hinder their ability to consistently assess the status of outstanding reprisal cases. According to federal internal control standards, monitoring of internal controls should be conducted to assess the quality of performance over time.[60] DODIG has responsibility for not only conducting its own investigations, but also for overseeing and approving the investigations conducted by service and other component IGs.[61] It can be challenging for DODIG to maintain visibility on all cases because a reprisal allegation can be made to and investigated by one of several IGs in DOD.

DODIG has not established standard monitoring processes and procedures and instead has been relying on ad hoc and inconsistent

---

[60] See: GAO/AIMD-00-21.3.1.

[61] Department of Defense Directive 7050.06 assigns those responsibilities to the DODIG and includes, within the definition of "DOD Components": the Office of the Secretary of Defense, the Military Departments, the Chairman of the Joint Chiefs of Staff, the Combatant Commands, the Office of the Inspector General of the Department of Defense, the Defense Agencies, the DOD Field Activities, and all other organizational entities within the Department of Defense.

GAO-12-362 Whistleblower Protection

efforts. For example, some service IG officials told us that they had not reconciled cases with the DODIG in several years and some service IG officials have recently been queried about cases that date back 5 years. DODIG and service officials told us that DODIG had not required service IGs to regularly report on the status of open cases. Additionally, our file review included a case where the DODIG identified an investigation begun by a service IG 6 years prior but never closed. DODIG was unable to establish contact with the complainant after 6 years and later administratively closed the case. Although this could be an extreme case, it may be indicative of a larger issue dealing with the tracking and management of complaints. Further, DODIG officials told us that the review of whistleblower reprisal cases involving senior level officials had in the past been handled by another office within DODIG and that the whistleblower reprisal directorate had limited visibility on the status of these cases. However, according to DODIG, it changed this procedure in late fiscal year 2011 so that the directorate responsible for whistleblower reprisal investigations also investigates or oversees service reprisal investigations involving senior officials. Moreover, DODIG's action plan outlines its approach to providing more consistent monitoring of all reprisal cases, including investigations of senior officials that include reprisal allegations. The first step in this plan has been to establish a team of investigators dedicated to providing oversight of service investigations. DODIG officials told us that once this team has worked through the backlog of cases, it will also implement more efforts to consistently monitor and reconcile cases to help ensure that all reprisal allegations are appropriately addressed in a timely manner. Until it further addresses the weaknesses in its monitoring practices of military whistleblower reprisal cases and the challenges it faces in its other oversight mechanisms, DODIG cannot be sure that it is adequately conducting its oversight responsibilities or implementing the whistleblower reprisal program as intended.

DOD Efforts to Ensure Corrective Actions Are Taken in Substantiated Cases Are Hindered by Disconnected Investigative and Corrective Action Processes and Unreliable Data

DOD's efforts to ensure that appropriate corrective action is taken after investigations are completed—both for whistleblowers and against those who reprise against whistleblowers—are hampered by disconnected investigative and corrective action processes and the limited visibility of corrective actions taken. Individuals with substantiated military whistleblower reprisal cases generally receive relief from the negative impacts caused by reprisal when they seek it from the BCMRs (80 percent of those who apply). However, few individuals with substantiated cases apply to the BCMRs for relief (19.1 percent). DODIG and the service BCMRs are also not consistently identifying and tracking data on corrective action taken to undo the damage done to the complainant by the reprisal. Further, unreliable data regarding corrective action taken against the subject are hindering oversight of this key aspect of whistleblower protection.

Few Servicemembers with Substantiated Cases Apply for the Relief Process

Most servicemembers with substantiated cases who seek relief from BCMRs receive it, but few apply for relief and so the secretaries of the military departments and the heads of the other DOD components are not generally able to take action to make the complainant whole in the vast majority of cases. The DOD directive governing the military whistleblower reprisal process, DOD Directive 7050.06, includes a largely service-centered process for obtaining corrective action that is separate from the investigative process centered on DODIG. Specifically, the directive charges the secretaries of the military departments and the heads of the other DOD components with taking corrective action based on the IG investigation.[62] Corrective action includes: (1) any action deemed necessary to make the complainant whole, (2) changes in agency regulations or practices, (3) administrative or disciplinary action against offending personnel, or (4) referral to the U.S. Attorney General or court-martial convening authority of any evidence of criminal violation. Although DODIG can investigate allegations of reprisal, makes all final determinations on investigations, and can make recommendations regarding appropriate corrective action, it does not have the authority to take corrective action, either for the complainant or against the subject. In order for servicemembers to receive relief from the negative impacts caused by reprisal—even for cases substantiated by DODIG—the law requires that servicemembers must file a separate application to their

---

[62] DOD Directive 7050.06 sections 5.3.3 and 5.4.2 (Jul. 23, 2007).

service BCMR.[63] For cases that are substantiated and those that are not, DODIG provides the appropriate service BCMR with the same case outcome notification it provides to the complainant. However, the DODIG notification letter does not automatically trigger a BCMR review of the case and/or corrective action.

For cases that servicemembers bring to the BCMRs, the Military Whistleblower Protection Act requires the BCMRs to review the whistleblower reprisal report approved by DODIG. However, BCMRs have authority to make independent determinations on military whistleblower reprisal cases and to engage in additional fact finding. Among other things, the statute also allows the BCMRs to request that DODIG or the service IGs gather additional evidence for the BCMR's consideration and hold hearings, although BCMR and DODIG officials told us that, to their knowledge, this authority had not ever been exercised. Further, it is up to the BCMR to make its own determination whether personnel action was in reprisal and recommend to the secretary of the military department appropriate actions to correct the record of those who have been reprised against. However, BCMR officials told us that they put significant credence in DODIG's findings and that their offices place a high priority on military whistleblower reprisal cases even though they make up only a small proportion of their total work.[64]

In our review of all substantiated reprisal cases submitted to BCMRs between fiscal year 2006 and the first half of fiscal year 2011, we found that the servicemembers with substantiated whistleblower reprisal allegations that applied for relief were generally successful in obtaining some relief.[65] Eighty percent of servicemembers (20 of 25) with substantiated reprisal cases—closed between fiscal year 2006 through the first half of 2011—who sought relief from a BCMR received some sort of remedy (see table 6).

---

[63] 10 U.S.C. §1034.

[64] Officials from each of the BCMRs told us that they review thousands of cases a year and that reprisal cases in any year run in the single digits.

[65] In this report, when we refer to the first half of fiscal year 2011, we mean between October 1, 2010 and March 31, 2011.

Table 6: Substantiated Reprisal Cases Submitted to BCMRs and Their Outcome for Cases Closed between Fiscal Year 2006 and the First Half of Fiscal Year 2011

BCMR	Cases submitted to BCMR by complainant	Cases where BCMR provided a remedy	Remedy provided (percent)
Air Force	9	9	100%
Army	6	3	50%
Navy (all)[a]	10	8	80%
Navy[a]	9	8	89%
Marine Corps[a]	1	0	—
Total	25	20	80%

Source: GAO analysis of DOD information.

Notes:

Based on DODIG data for cases that included military whistleblower reprisal allegations substantiated by DODIG between October 1, 2005 and March 31, 2011, and BCMR data regarding the cases submitted to them, including case outcome.

Data do not include cases in which, according to DODIG data, the military whistleblower reprisal allegations were not substantiated but an improper referral for mental health evaluation (IMHE) was substantiated. Including those figures boosts the total number of cases submitted to the BCMRs to 31 and boosts the number of cases where the BCMR provided a remedy to 25, or 81 percent.

The Navy BCMR reviews cases for the Department of the Navy and therefore handles cases from both Navy personnel and Marine Corps personnel.

Two cases (one Army, one Marine Corps) in which a complainant submitted an application to a BCMR were not included because the BCMRs had not yet completed action on them.

Remedy provided indicates that the complainant received at least partial remedy. It does not indicate that the complainants received the exact remedy they were seeking.

[a]Two Navy BCMR cases—one from the Marine Corps and one from the Navy—were included and considered as not having received remedy although the Navy BCMR data are unclear whether or not it provided remedy. If the Navy BCMR provided remedy in these cases, then all Navy and Marine Corps substantiated whistleblower reprisal allegations brought before the BCMR received some remedy.

The most common corrective action taken by the services in response to applications filed by complainants with substantiated military whistleblower reprisal allegations was amending or removing a rating from the complainant's personnel record. This occurred in 14 of the 25 substantiated cases brought to the BCMRs. For example, in 1of the cases a servicemember with a substantiated whistleblower reprisal case requested that the Army BCMR remove two ratings from his record. The Army BCMR decided to remove the one rating that the DODIG found was done in reprisal. The second most common corrective action taken by the services was providing payment, benefits, awards, or training that was denied as a result of the reprisal. This occurred in 6 of the 25 substantiated cases brought to the BCMRs. For example, in one of the cases, a servicemember was given a Bronze Star that had been denied to him because of a reprisal. The third most common corrective action taken by the services was amending or removing disciplinary actions from an individual's personnel record. For example, the Air Force BCMR removed a letter of reprimand from a servicemember's file that DODIG found was a result of an act of reprisal. This occurred in 4 of the 25 substantiated cases brought to the BCMRs. There were also a number of cases where the service took more than one corrective action. For example, a Navy petty officer had a disciplinary action removed from his record, a promotion backdated, and retroactive pay instated to go along with the backdated promotion.

Although 80 percent of servicemembers with substantiated whistleblower reprisal allegations who applied for relief received some relief, only about 1 in 5 servicemembers with whistleblower reprisal allegations substantiated by DODIG applied to the BCMRs for relief during the time period we reviewed. As shown in table 7, only 25 of the 131 (19.1 percent) of complainants with substantiated cases submitted applications for relief with their BCMR. As a result, only 15 percent of servicemembers with reprisal allegations substantiated by DODIG received some relief through their BCMRs. We found that there were differences between the services regarding the proportion of cases submitted to the BCMRs, with more than half of the substantiated Navy cases being brought to the Navy BCMR and only approximately 1 in 10 substantiated Army cases being brought to the Army BCMR.

Table 7: Substantiated Reprisal Cases Submitted to BCMRs Compared to All Substantiated Cases for Cases Closed Between Fiscal Year 2006 and the First Half of Fiscal Year 2011

BCMR	Total cases substantiated	Cases submitted to BCMR by complainant	Cases where BCMR provided a remedy	Percentage of total cases substantiated	
				Case submitted	Remedy provided
Air Force	58	9	9	15.5%	15.5%
Army	54	6	3	11.1%	5.6%
Navy (all)[a]	19	10	8	52.6%	42.1%
Navy[a]	17	9	8	52.9%	47.1%
Marine Corps[a]	2	1	0	50%	0
Total	131	25	20	19.1%	15.3%

Source: GAO analysis of DOD information.

Notes:

Based on DODIG data for cases that included military whistleblower reprisal allegations substantiated by DODIG between October 1, 2005 and March 31, 2011, and BCMR data regarding the cases submitted to them, including case outcome.

Total substantiated cases do not include two cases (one Army, one Marine Corps) in which a complainant submitted an application to a BCMR because the BCMRs had not yet completed action on them. It also does not include 2 Army cases that, according to data provided by the Army BCMR, DODIG misidentified in their database as containing substantiated whistleblower reprisal claims when they had substantiated only improper referral for mental health evaluations (IMHE).

Data does not include cases in which, according to DODIG data, the military whistleblower reprisal allegations are not substantiated but an improper referral for mental health evaluation (IMHE) is substantiated. Including those figures does not significantly impact total cases submitted—the percent changes from 19.1 percent to 19.0 percent. Total remedy provided is 15.3 percent in both cases.

The Navy BCMR reviews cases for the Department of the Navy and therefore handles cases from both Navy personnel and Marine Corps personnel.

There were 9 cases in which complainants did not apply to the Army BCMR for record correction where the BCMR could not have provided relief had the complainant applied. The BCMR could not have provided relief because the substantiated claim did not impact the complainant's record. For example, the complainant was threatened with adverse action or was restricted from making a lawful communication to an IG or Member of Congress. Neither action would result in a negative impact on the complainant's personnel file. Not counting these Army cases would change the Army cases submitted and Army remedy provided to 13.3 percent and 6.7 percent, respectively. It would also change the total cases submitted and total remedy provided to 20.5 percent and 16.4 percent, respectively. We did not identify similar circumstances for cases processed by the Air Force and Navy BCMRs based on the information provided by these organizations.

Remedy provided indicates that complainants received at least partial remedy. It does not indicate that complainants received the exact remedy they were seeking.

[a]Two Navy BCMR cases—one from the Marine Corps and one from the Navy—were included and considered as not having received remedy, although the Navy BCMR data are unclear whether or not it provided remedy. If the Navy BCMR provided remedy in these cases, then all Navy and Marine Corps substantiated whistleblower reprisal allegations brought before the BCMR received some remedy.

Officials from DODIG, the service IGs, and the BCMRs indicated that they did not know the exact reason why so few servicemembers with substantiated reprisal allegations apply for relief. There are some cases for which the BCMRs cannot provide relief. For example, a BCMR cannot correct the record for an individual where DODIG substantiated that the individual was threatened with reprisal but where no actual harm was done to that individual's record. Similarly, a BCMR cannot correct the record for an individual where DODIG substantiated that the individual was restricted from making a lawful communication to an IG in DOD or Member of Congress. We identified nine Army cases where the Army BCMR was not in a position to provide relief. Discounting those nine cases would increase the percentage of servicemembers with substantiated claims that submitted cases to the Army BCMR from 11.1 percent to 13.3 percent (see table 7 and associated notes for further details). However, the overall impact of such cases appears to be minimal due to the relatively low number of substantiated cases involving only restriction or threats of reprisal.[66] Officials from the Air Force and Army BCMRs also said that some servicemembers may be seeking relief from other lower-level service boards, such as the Air Force Evaluation Report Appeals Board or the Army's Enlisted Special Review Board, even though servicemembers are told in their letter from DODIG to obtain relief from the BCMRs. The officials did not know of any such incidents but said it was a possibility. Data obtained from the Army BCMR shows four such incidents, with the other board providing relief to the servicemember in one of the four cases. Discounting those four cases would increase the percentage of servicemembers with substantiated claims that submitted cases to the Army BCMR from 11.1 percent to 12.0 percent.[67] Based on these data, the impact of complainants taking cases to boards other than BCMR is relatively modest and does not explain the large difference between the number of substantiated cases and the number of cases brought to the BCMRs.

Service and DODIG officials also stated that the length of time it takes for servicemembers to get their reprisal allegations substantiated may impact their willingness to engage in yet another process. Servicemembers frequently rotate to other assignments at different locations around the world and so could be in a completely new work environment with a different chain of command by the time the reprisal investigation is completed. The officials also said that servicemembers may have left the service during the time it takes to substantiate a claim. Our case file review included a nongeneralizable subset of seven substantiated whistleblower reprisal cases that took a mean of 614 days to close and with a range of 439 days to 796 days. Only one of the seven servicemembers with a substantiated case from our file review applied for relief with their BCMR, and DODIG took 750 days to substantiate that one claim.

---

[66] Our review of a random sample of case files closed between January 1, 2009 and March 31, 2011, found one case where restriction was substantiated and one where the threat of an unfavorable personnel action was substantiated. Neither complainant brought their case to a BCMR for review and remedy.

[67] Data obtained from the Air Force BCMR showed that the Air Force Evaluation Report Appeals Board provided partial remedy to one applicant who had a military whistleblower reprisal case substantiated by DODIG between fiscal year 2006 and the first half of 2011. However, that applicant also obtained additional remedy from the Air Force BCMR.

A further factor that could impact the willingness of those with substantiated reprisal claims from pursuing remedy from their service BCMR is a lack of understanding regarding the available remedies. The Military Whistleblower Protection Act allows a report of investigation to include recommendations regarding the corrective action. According to DODIG's investigative guide, recommendations should be made if there is a substantiated reprisal allegation. It states that recommendations can be general or specific but that the corrective action "should be sufficient to make the complainant 'whole' and restore the complainant to the same or equal status he or she would have attained if the reprisal had not occurred." According to DODIG officials, DODIG used to provide detailed recommendations regarding what it thought would be appropriate remedies for the complainant. For example, the 1996 investigative guide includes an example of a case that recommends a specific evaluation report be voided and the complainant be reinstated to his former position or one commensurate to it. Nevertheless, DODIG's current practice is to provide a more general recommendation that appropriate corrective action be taken. DODIG officials did not know when or why this change in practice occurred but acknowledged that it would be appropriate and helpful to provide more detailed recommendations for how to make the complainant whole. Without knowing more about when and how this practice changed, we were not able to identify if there is an association between the level of detail in recommendations and the proportion of individuals who apply to the BCMRs. However, it is reasonable to assume that without detailing in the investigative report the types of remedies that could be appropriate, the servicemember may not be aware of the full benefit realized by applying for relief to the BCMR.

Service BCMRs Are Not Consistently Identifying Reprisal Cases

The service BCMRs are not consistently identifying applicants who have substantiated reprisal cases as such and are therefore not providing all reprisal victims with the procedural privileges to which they are entitled. The Military Whistleblower Protection Act[68] provides whistleblowers with unique procedural privileges that are generally not afforded to other applicants to the BCMRs. These privileges include:

---

[68] 10 U.S.C. § 1034, as amended.

1. direct application for corrective action may be made to the service BCMR instead of first going to a lower level of administrative appeal;[69]
2. 180-day deadline for the BCMR to review and the secretary of the military department concerned to render a final decision in the case, which differs from other cases processed by BCMRs; and
3. right to appeal BCMR decisions to the Secretary of Defense.[70]

Further, according to federal internal control standards, agencies need operating information to determine whether they are achieving their compliance requirements under various laws and regulations.[71] BCMR officials also told us that whistleblower reprisal cases are high-priority cases for the BCMRs, even though they receive only a few a year compared to the many thousands of other cases they process. They therefore make a special effort to track reprisal cases.[72]

Although the Military Whistleblower Protection Act provides unique procedural privileges to whistleblowers who apply to BCMRs for relief, the BCMRs are not consistently identifying applicants with substantiated whistleblower reprisal cases as such and are therefore not always aware

---

[69] The BCMRs are the highest level of administrative review in the services.

[70] According to BCMR officials, servicemembers with cases that are not whistleblower reprisal have to challenge BCMR decisions in federal court.

[71] GAO/AIMD-00-21.3.1.

[72] The service BCMRs have adopted different interpretations of what cases qualify as a reprisal case. DOD Directive 7050.06 requires secretaries of the military departments to ensure that BCMRs shall consider applications for the correction of military records at the request of servicemembers or former servicemembers who allege that they have been reprised against due to their whistleblower activity. The Air Force BCMR considers anyone with a reasonable whistleblower reprisal claim to be a whistleblower with the corresponding procedural privileges. The Army and Navy BCMRs consider only applicants with cases substantiated by DODIG as whistleblowers. Other cases that may include whistleblower allegations that are not substantiated are reviewed under each BCMR's regular authority. Army officials added that, should the Army BCMR ultimately determine that an applicant's reprisal case has merit even if it was not substantiated by DODIG, the Army BCMR has the ability to invoke its authority under the Military Whistleblower Reprisal Act.

when these procedural privileges should apply.[73] We found that the BCMRs did not identify 10 of the 25 applicants with whistleblower reprisal cases substantiated by DODIG as whistleblower reprisal cases (see table 8). Additionally, we found in the aggregate that cases that are not identified as whistleblower reprisal cases took longer. This was true for each BCMR but was more pronounced with the Navy BCMR. Data provided by the Navy BCMR showed that it processed in 40 days (mean) the six cases that were identified as reprisal in their database but took 235 days (mean) to process four cases not identified as reprisal (see app. III). Between those cases identified as reprisal and those that were not, we did not observe a difference in overall proportion of applicants who were provided remedy by the BCMRs. However, complainants who do not receive remedy or are not satisfied by the remedy they received from the BCMR and who the BCMR did not identify as a whistleblower reprisal case are not informed of their right to appeal to the Secretary of Defense. Instead, these individuals are treated as non-whistleblower applicants and so told that their administrative appeals options have been exhausted within the service, unless they have new information to provide to the BCMRs. The applicants are also advised that they may seek remedy in a court of appropriate jurisdiction.

---

[73] In GAO/NSIAD-95-23, *Whistleblower Protection: Continuing Impediments to Protection of Military Members* (February 1995), we reported that at that time BCMRs were unable to identify any specific whistleblower cases because they were not uniquely coding them. As a result of a settlement in a 1977 court action, DOD and service directives required the BCMRs to establish a single index system for all BCMR cases except those involving characterizations of discharge. The system was to provide a means for applicants to identify or isolate cases that may be similar to theirs and indicate the grounds for which the BCMR or Secretary granted or denied relief. The Department of the Army was responsible for developing the initial format of the index system, establishing joint facilities for inspection, and copying opinions. We therefore recommended that the BCMRs establish the required code. According to Army BCMR officials, in 2002 the court approved DOD's request to discontinue standardized BCMR indexing of cases because the new data systems used by the BCMRs fulfilled the underlying purpose for the court order.

Table 8: Comparison of Substantiated Cases Identified and Not Identified as Reprisal by the BCMRs (for Cases Closed between Fiscal Year 2006 and the First Half of Fiscal Year 2011)

	All reprisal cases submitted to BCMR	Cases identified by BCMR reprisal	Cases not identified by BCMR as reprisal
Number of cases	25	15	10
Percent of all cases	100%	60%	40%
Mean days to close case	179	133	249
Cases over 180 days	9	4	5
Percent of cases over 180 days	36%	27%	50%
Remedy provided	20	12	8
Percent remedy provided	80%	80%	80%

Source: GAO analysis of DOD information.

Notes:

Based on DODIG data for cases that included military whistleblower reprisal allegations substantiated by DODIG between October 1, 2005 and March 31, 2011, and BCMR data regarding the cases submitted to them, including case outcome.

The Navy BCMR reviews cases for the Department of the Navy and therefore handles cases from both Navy personnel and Marine Corps personnel.

Two cases (one Army, one Marine Corps) in which a complainant submitted an application to a BCMR were not included because the BCMRs had not yet completed action on them.

Two Navy BCMR cases—one from the Marine Corps and one from the Navy—were included and considered as not having received remedy, although the Navy BCMR data are unclear whether or not it provided remedy. The Marine Corps case was not identified by the Navy BCMR as being a military whistleblower reprisal case. The Navy case was identified as a military whistleblower reprisal case.

A more detailed table by service can be found in app. III.

Remedy provided indicates that the complainant received at least partial remedy. It does not indicate that the complainant received the exact remedy they were seeking.

We identified two factors that may impact the ability to consistently identify substantiated military whistleblower reprisal cases across all of the service BCMRs. First, service BCMR officials told us that they may not be properly identifying all whistleblower reprisal cases in their case tracking system because it is not always readily apparent on a complainant's application that it is a whistleblower case. The form used by whistleblowers to apply for relief from a BCMR is the same general form used by all applicants to the BCMRs. This form requires a narrative description and does not have a special indicator, such as a checkbox, to identify the case as a whistleblower reprisal case. The officials said that their intake organizations and reviewers could therefore miss that an applicant is a whistleblower if the applicant did not explicitly mention it.

Second, the different approaches service BCMRs take to DODIG notifications of substantiated cases they receive may also impact how consistently they identify military whistleblower reprisal cases. The success of identifying military whistleblower reprisal cases varies by service BCMR, with the Army properly identifying 83 percent of the cases (5 of 6), the Navy identifying 60 percent of the cases (6 of 10), and the Air Force identifying 44 percent of the cases (4 of 9) for cases closed between fiscal year 2006 and the first half of fiscal year 2011 (see app. III). Army BCMR officials told us that a method they used to identify military whistleblower reprisal cases is to create an electronic case file for every substantiated case notification they receive from DODIG. Although they immediately close the case in the database, it acts as a flag to identify a case as a whistleblower reprisal case should a complainant apply to the Army BCMR for relief. The Air Force and Navy BCMRs do not have a similar procedure. By not properly identifying a significant proportion of whistleblower reprisal cases as reprisal cases, the BCMRs are not providing all whistleblower applicants with the unique procedural privileges afforded them by law.

Unreliable Data Limits Visibility and Oversight of Corrective Action

DODIG lacks reliable data on the corrective action taken in response to substantiated whistleblower reprisal cases, which limits the visibility and oversight DOD and Congress have of the final portion of the military whistleblower reprisal process. According to federal internal control standards, oversight mechanisms are an integral part of an entity's planning, implementing, reviewing, and accountability for stewardship of government resources and achieving effective results.[74] Oversight mechanisms include the policies, procedures, techniques, and mechanisms that enforce management's directives and help ensure that actions are taken to address risks. The impact of whistleblower reprisal investigations comes with the corrective actions taken in response to substantiated cases. Additionally, the 2009 Department of Justice review recommended that the results of investigations that substantiate allegations of reprisal be publicized as a way to heighten awareness within the services of the Military Whistleblower Protection Act, to potentially deter future incidents of reprisal, and to possibly encourage other reprisal victims to come forward.

---

[74] GAO/AIMD-00-21.3.1.

While DODIG cannot directly take corrective action in response to a substantiated case, it is the focal point for DOD's military whistleblower reprisal program and is well positioned to collect and monitor data regarding program outcomes. DODIG has a directorate dedicated primarily to whistleblower reprisal allegation investigations and designated to receive information from the military departments on corrective action, so is well positioned not only to collect the information on corrective action but also to use that information to help enhance oversight of the military whistleblower reprisal process and ensure that it is achieving effective results. DODIG officials stated that because DODIG is the focal point for DOD's military whistleblower reprisal activities, it is important for them to have visibility and information of all military whistleblower reprisal activities, not only to provide oversight but also to provide a central place within the department where internal and external stakeholders can obtain information. They explained that they would want to know, for example, if complainants were having difficulty obtaining corrective action so that they could try to address such a problem. They also noted that it was important to have complete data since Members of Congress come to DODIG for information on military whistleblower reprisal activities. The officials emphasized that understanding the relevance of their investigative work depends on knowing what corrective action was taken in response to that work.

Although DODIG officials acknowledge the importance of information on corrective action, the service BCMRs are not consistently reporting and DODIG is not maintaining data on the actions BCMRs take in response to reprisal cases. DOD Directive 7050.06 requires the secretaries of the military departments to notify DODIG and the service IG concerned of decisions in regards to applications from whistleblower reprisal complainants for the correction of military records.[75] BCMR officials told us that they are supposed to provide this notification on behalf of the service secretary but have not been consistently carrying out this responsibility. DODIG officials also told us that they are not aware of receiving any BCMR reports regarding case outcomes. However, DODIG also did not follow up with the services regarding this information because it had chosen not to track this information. DODIG therefore has had no visibility into or oversight capacity for this portion of the military whistleblower reprisal program. During the course of our review, however,

---

[75] DOD Directive 7050.06, Section 5.3.8 (July 23, 2007).

DODIG officials acknowledged that they should be collecting and monitoring information on corrective action provided to whistleblowers and stated that they would begin doing so as part of their ongoing reforms to the whistleblower reprisal process.

DOD has a separate process for taking and tracking corrective action against those who have reprised against whistleblowers—also called command action. DOD Directive 7050.06 directs the secretaries of the military departments and the heads of the other DOD components to take corrective action based on the IG reports of investigations of military whistleblower reprisal allegations, and to notify DODIG of the action taken within 10 working days.[76] Further, DODIG requires that the service IGs report back to DODIG on command action taken against the subject—the individual alleged to have reprised against a whistleblower—according to officials from these organizations. DODIG records command action taken in its database and has reported in its semiannual reports to Congress examples of command action taken in response to substantiated military whistleblower reprisal claims.

While DOD Directive 7050.06 ultimately places responsibility for taking corrective action on the secretaries of the military departments based on the DODIG findings, it is up to a subject's military commanding officer to determine whether command action against the subject is appropriate, and if so, what form it should take. Military commanders are responsible for good order and discipline in their commands, and they have a number of judicial and administrative options at their disposal. DODIG officials told us that if a commander takes action against a subject in a military whistleblower reprisal case, it is largely, if not exclusively, an administrative action. Administrative actions are the least severe of the categories of command action available to the commander and can range from verbal counseling to written reprimands and demotion.

Although DODIG has an important role in collecting information on and monitoring command action taken against subjects in response to substantiated whistleblower reprisal cases, DODIG has not been maintaining in its database reliable information on command action needed to fulfill this role. Specifically, DODIG data on command action indicates that almost half of all substantiated cases (40 percent) that were

---

[76] DOD Directive 7050.06 Sections 5.3.3 and 5.4.2 (July 23, 2007).

closed from October 1, 2005 through March 31, 2011, were awaiting reports from the services regarding the command action taken. According to most of the service IGs, they are diligent in providing command action information to DODIG on a timely basis. Data provided by the services showed that there were no cases pending follow-up action but we determined that the service data were not reliable enough for our purposes. However, DODIG officials also acknowledged that their information on command action was incomplete and that they were taking steps to both supplement data on existing closed cases and collect and maintain reliable data for command action taken in response to future substantiated cases. Until DODIG has reliable data on corrective action, DOD and Congress will be hindered in their ability to provide oversight of the corrective action portion of the military whistleblower reprisal program.

Conclusions

Whistleblowers play an important role in safeguarding the federal government against waste, fraud, and abuse, and Congress has enacted legislation to provide military whistleblowers with protections against reprisal. The requirements of the Military Whistleblower Protection Act provide complainants with a means to redress wrongs committed against them as a result of their whistleblowing; establish processes for holding subjects accountable; and provide the Secretary of Defense and decision makers with visibility over the military whistleblower reprisal investigative process and its outcomes. Recognizing problems with the process, and in response to its own internal review and a Department of Justice report it requested, the DODIG has expressed a renewed commitment to meeting the statutory timeliness and reporting requirements and ensuring quality investigations. Further, it has taken some steps to achieve these goals and to improve oversight of its investigations into allegations of reprisal against whistleblowers. Additional actions are needed, however. For example, recording, collecting, and tracking accurate, relevant data on case processing times would aid DOD in its efforts to identify inefficiencies or challenges to meeting timeliness requirements and in reporting to internal and external stakeholders. Finalizing the development and implementation of performance metrics for whistleblower reprisal investigations, such as ensuring case files contain evidence sufficient to support conclusions, would provide DOD with a means of ensuring that DOD is meeting its own standards for completing quality investigations. In addition, oversight actions—such as updating and adhering to the guidance governing investigations—could help improve the quality and oversight of reprisal cases. Finally, the overall purpose of DOD's whistleblower reprisal program is to identify servicemembers who have been reprised against, make them whole, and ensure that there are appropriate consequences for those who reprised against the whistleblower. This could be furthered if the DODIG and the service BCMRs develop processes and procedures to facilitate consideration of all substantiated allegations by the appropriate service BCMR. Increasing the completeness and reliability of data on corrective action could also provide DOD and Congress with information they need for oversight. Without addressing these issues, military whistleblowers may not be getting the full protection and resolution they deserve and DOD may not be reaping the full benefits whistleblowers could provide the department.

Recommendations for Executive Action

To assist DOD with improving processing times of these investigations, we recommend that the Secretary of Defense work in coordination with DODIG to:

- implement policies and procedures to ensure accurate and complete recording and consistent tracking of total case processing time and processing time for various phases of the investigation;
- track and analyze timeliness data to identify reforms that could aid in processing cases within the 180 days provided by law; and
- regularly report to Congress on the timeliness of military whistleblower reprisal investigations, including the number of cases exceeding the 180 days provided by law. DODIG could do so in its semiannual reports.

To assist DOD in improving oversight over the whistleblower reprisal investigative process, we recommend that the Secretary of Defense work in coordination with DODIG to:

- develop and implement performance metrics to ensure the quality and effectiveness of the investigative process, such as ensuring that the case files contain evidence sufficient to support the conclusions;
- update whistleblower reprisal investigative guidance and ensure that it is consistently followed, including clarifying reporting requirements, responsibilities, and terminology; and
- consistently monitor the status of whistleblower reprisal investigations.

DODIG should work in close consultation with the service IGs when implementing these recommendations.

To better ensure that whistleblowers obtain the relief they are due, we recommend that the Secretary of Defense work in coordination with DODIG to identify best practices and develop the necessary processes and procedures to ensure that all whistleblower reprisal allegations substantiated by DODIG are considered under the whistleblower statute by the appropriate service BCMR. For example, DODIG could provide more detailed recommendations regarding corrective action for the complainant. DODIG should work in close consultation with the service IGs and the BCMRs when implementing this recommendation.

To ensure that the BCMRs are treating military whistleblower reprisal cases appropriately, given the unique procedural privileges provided by the Military Whistleblower Protection Act, we recommend that the Secretary of Defense direct the secretaries of the military departments to take action to ensure that military whistleblower cases are correctly identified and processed by the BCMRs. Such actions could include modifying the form used to apply to the BCMR; additional training so that BCMR staff can better identify cases; or developing methods for identifying cases for which the BCMRs have received DODIG substantiated case notifications.

To assist DOD in improving oversight of all corrective action taken in response to substantiated military whistleblower reprisal claims, including command action, we recommend that the Secretary of Defense work in coordination with DODIG to:

- establish standardized corrective action reporting requirements;
- consistently track and regularly reconcile data regarding corrective action; and
- regularly report to Congress on the frequency and type of corrective action taken in response to substantiated reprisal claims. DODIG could do so, for example, in its semiannual reports to Congress.

DODIG should work in concert with the service IGs and BCMRs when implementing these recommendations.

Agency Comments and Our Evaluation

In commenting on a draft of this report, DOD concurred with each of our recommendations. DOD's comments are reprinted in appendix IV. DOD also provided technical comments, which we considered and incorporated where appropriate.

In concurring with our recommendations that DODIG implement policies and procedures to ensure accurate and complete tracking of total case processing times and processing time for various phases of the investigation, track and analyze timeliness data, and regularly report to

Congress on the timeliness of military whistleblower reprisal investigations, DOD stated that DODIG recognized the necessity of policies and procedures to ensure accurate and complete tracking of processing time for all phases of investigations and was taking multiple steps to address the GAO recommendations. These steps include modifying internal processes and updating policy manuals, redesigning the case management database, relying on data analysis to evaluate reforms and identifying further reforms, and reporting timeliness data to Congress. We believe that these steps, when fully implemented, could provide the department and the Congress with enhanced visibility over the status of military whistleblower reprisal investigations.

In concurring with our recommendations that DODIG develop and implement performance metrics, update and consistently follow guidance, and consistently monitor the status of military whistleblower reprisal cases, DOD stated that DODIG is taking steps to address each one of these areas, including revising its manual for administrative investigations to include clearly defined performance metrics, the required contents of investigative case files, as well as defining reporting requirements, responsibilities, and relevant terminology. It has also established a new oversight team which reviews and approves the determinations reached by the service IGs. DODIG is also in the process of establishing procedures that will directly monitor the progress of investigations and track command actions taken. We believe that the steps that DOD noted in its response could improve DOD's means of ensuring that DOD is meeting its own standards for completing quality investigations.

In concurring with our recommendation that DODIG, in close consultation with the service IGs and the BCMRs, identify best practices and develop the necessary process and procedures to ensure that all substantiated military whistleblower reprisal cases are considered by the appropriate BCMR, DOD stated that the mentioned organizations will begin meeting together within the next six weeks to identify best practices and develop an effective way forward. We acknowledge the department's stated commitment to these steps and encourage it to work toward the broad range of recommended steps, including that DODIG provide more detailed recommendations regarding corrective action for complainants.

In concurring with our recommendation that the service BCMRs take action to ensure that military whistleblower reprisal cases are correctly identified and processed by the BCMRs, DOD stated that the BCMRs will consider how to best ensure that whistleblowers with substantiated reprisal complaints are provided with all the information they need to determine if an application to a BCMR is appropriate. Although providing information to whistleblowers is a positive step, this alone will not address our finding that the service BCMRs are not consistently identifying applicants who have substantiated reprisal cases as such and are therefore not providing all reprisal victims with the procedural privileges to which they are entitled. Our recommendation included examples of possible actions the BCMRs could take to ensure that they are correctly identifying cases, including modifying the application form, additional training for BCMR staff, or developing methods for using the DODIG notification to BCMRs of substantiated cases as a way to flag military whistleblower reprisal cases, much like the Army BCMR does. We believe that improving the BCMRs' ability to properly identify substantiated military whistleblower reprisal cases could help to ensure that such cases are properly considered under the military whistleblower statute by the appropriate service BCMR.

In concurring with our recommendations that DODIG establish standardized corrective action reporting requirements, track and reconcile such data, and regularly report such information to Congress, DOD indicated that DODIG is redesigning its case management database to better enable it to record and report on such information. The overall purpose of DOD's whistleblower reprisal program is to identify servicemembers who have been reprised against, make them whole, and ensure that there are appropriate consequences for those who reprised against the whistleblower. We believe that the department's stated commitment to collecting and maintaining reliable data on corrective action—both for the remedies provided to complainants and command actions taken against subjects—and also regularly reporting such information to Congress could enhance oversight of the outcomes of the military whistleblower reprisal program.

We are sending copies of this report to the appropriate congressional committees. We are also sending copies to the Secretary of Defense. In addition, the report is available at no charge on the GAO website at http://www.gao.gov.

If you or your staff have any questions about this report, please contact me at (202) 512-5257 or merrittz@gao.gov. Contact points for our Offices of Congressional Relations and Public Affairs may be found on the last page of this report. GAO staff who made key contributions to this report are listed in appendix V.

Zina Merritt
Director
Defense Capabilities and Management

Appendix I: Scope and Methodology

During our review of the Department of Defense's (DOD) military whistleblower reprisal program, we reviewed relevant documentation, gathered and assessed data, and met with representatives from numerous agencies, including the DOD Inspector General (DODIG), and Inspector General (IG) officials from the services (Army, Navy, Air Force, and Marine Corps). Table 9 lists all of the organizations we met with during our review. To determine DOD's process for investigating military whistleblower reprisals cases, we reviewed documents outlining investigative processes of DODIG and service IGs, including DODIG's investigative guide, and agency briefings and memoranda, and we spoke with officials from those organizations.[1]

Table 9: Organizations Met with During Review

Organization	Interviews conducted
DODIG	The Inspector General of the Department of Defense, Administrative Investigations, Office of Communications and Congressional Liaison, Whistleblower Reprisal Investigations Directorate,[a] Office of General Counsel, Office of Whistleblowing and Transparency
Army	Department of the Army Inspector General, Army National Guard Bureau Inspector General, U.S. Army Forces Command Inspector General, Army Board for Correction of Military Records
Air Force	Secretary of the Air Force Inspector General, Air Combat Command Inspector General, Air Force Reserve Command Inspector General, Global Strike Command Inspector General, Pacific Air Forces Inspector General, US Air Forces Europe Inspector General, 11 Wing Inspector General, Air Force Board for Correction of Military Records
Navy	Naval Inspector General; Commander, Navy Installations Command Inspector General; U.S. Fleet Forces Command Inspector General; Commander, Navy Reserve Forces Command Inspector General; Board for Correction of Naval Records
Marine Corps	Marine Corps Inspector General, Marine Corps Training and Education Command Inspector General, Marine Corps Third Marine Aircraft Wing Inspector General
Office of the Secretary of Defense	Office of the Under Secretary of Defense for Personnel and Readiness – Enterprise Services

Source: GAO.

[a]DODIG formed the Whistleblower Reprisal Investigations directorate during the course of our review when it merged the Military Reprisal Investigations and Civilian Reprisal Investigations directorates. We had previously met with the Military Reprisal Investigations directorate.

[1] DOD Inspector General Departmental Guidance 7050.6, *Guide to Investigating Reprisal and Improper Referrals for Mental Health Evaluations,* (Feb. 6, 1996).

Two primary sources of data used in several of our objectives were military whistleblower reprisal data from DODIG's database and from a random selection of DODIG closed military whistleblower reprisal case files. DODIG provided us with information for all military whistleblower reprisal cases opened and closed between fiscal year 2006 and the first half of fiscal year 2011 from the two databases they used to record these data.[2] We combined the information from the two databases into one complete dataset, eliminating duplicate cases as per directions provided by DODIG. We also consulted with DODIG officials to ensure that we were properly identifying the various data elements. In addition, we based our case file selection on the consolidated dataset of DODIG military whistleblower reprisal data. Specifically, a GAO statistician determined that a random sample of 97 cases from a list of the 871 military whistleblower reprisal cases DODIG closed between January 1, 2009 and March 31, 2011, would be appropriate. Our sample size of 97 cases was chosen to be generalizable, with a margin of error of 10 percentage points at the 95 percent confidence level for percentage estimates. We chose this time period because it represented DOD's most recent efforts and because DODIG had these files on site.[3] Based on our review of whistleblower reprisal policies and procedures, we created a data collection instrument to identify the key characteristics of whistleblower reprisal cases, check the data reliability of the database information, and assess the completeness of files. We also developed a standard approach to reviewing files to ensure we reviewed all cases consistently. We refined this data collection instrument and our approach by first reviewing 12 case files that were not part of the 97 identified. Our methodology for reviewing the random sample required two analysts to review each case file, enter the information for each field in the data collection instrument, and transfer their information for each case to a

---

[2] At the time DODIG provided us the data, it kept information on reprisal cases in two databases. DODIG used the CASES database to record information for all cases that it investigated and those cases that went to full investigation. DODIG used the separate Service IG Reprisal Case (SIRC) database to record information on military whistleblower reprisal cases reviewed by the service IGs. However, if those service cases went to full investigation, DODIG would close the case in SIRC and reopen the case in CASES. In October 2011, DODIG began phasing out the use of its SIRC database by recording information on all new cases in its CASES database. Although DODIG used two databases to record information, in this report we generally refer to the information from these databases as data from the DODIG database (singular).

[3] DODIG officials stated that their file retention policy is to keep files on site for the current year and the 2 previous calendar years before files are sent to an off-site archive.

central spreadsheet. We compared the two scores for each case, and highlighted the elements for which there was disagreement. Reviewers discussed the areas of disagreement and resolved any differences by identifying the necessary evidence in the case files. During the course of the case file review, our original sample size was reduced from 97 to 91 because 3 of the cases were found to be ongoing investigations, 2 cases were not military whistleblower reprisal cases, and DODIG could not locate 1 of the case files. However, this reduced sample is still generalizable, with an 11 percent margin of error at the 95 percent confidence level. Case file review results based on probability samples are subject to sampling error. The sample we drew for our case file review is only one of a large number of samples we might have drawn. Because different samples could have provided different estimates, we express our confidence in the precision of our particular sample results as a 95 percent confidence interval. This is the interval that would contain the actual population values for 95 percent of the samples we could have drawn. As a result, we are 95 percent confident that each of the confidence intervals in this report will include the true values in the study population. The margin of error associated with the confidence intervals of our case file review proportion estimates is no more than plus or minus 11 percentage points at the 95 percent level of confidence. The margin of error for any mean values based on our case file review will vary depending on the variability of the data and so is reported along with the mean.

In order to determine the extent to which DOD is meeting timeliness requirements for investigating military whistleblower reprisals, we reviewed relevant documents including The Military Whistleblower Protection Act, and its implementing directive on military whistleblower protections, DOD Directive 7050.06, *Military Whistleblower Protection* (Jul. 23, 2007). To identify possible challenges DOD faces in meeting these requirements, we reviewed key documents, including internal agency memos and briefings; the July 2009 Department of Justice Inspector General report; *A Review of the Department of Defense Office of Inspector General's Process for Handling Military Whistleblower Reprisal Allegations*; and DODIG's May 2011 *Review of the Office of Deputy Inspector General for Administrative Investigations, Directorate for Military Reprisal Investigations*. We also reviewed the 2010 DODIG report to Congress on progress made regarding recommendations from the Department of Justice review, and DODIG's October 2011 action plan in order to identify the steps DODIG has taken to address timeliness challenges. In order to determine if DOD was meeting statutory timeliness and reporting requirements, we conducted analysis of 91 randomly selected case files for cases closed between January 1, 2009 and March 31, 2011, (see above) and recorded the opening and closing dates indicated in the documentation for each case. We further reviewed those case files for evidence regarding timeliness reporting requirements. In order to determine the reliability of timeliness information in DODIG's database, we compared the opening and closing dates we determined by reviewing the case files to the opening and closing dates recorded for those cases in DODIG's database. We conducted checks to see whether DODIG database timeliness fields were filled out to determine if DODIG had reliable information on the time it takes to complete various investigative phases. In addition, we spoke with officials from DODIG and officials from the service IGs and the Office of the Under Secretary of Defense for Personnel and Readiness – Enterprise Services regarding timeliness issues, including compliance with timeliness reporting requirements.

In order to assess DODIG's actions to address overall process internal controls, we interviewed and discussed with DODIG officials their efforts to improve oversight of the whistleblower reprisal program. We also examined DODIG documents, including an internal review of the whistleblower reprisal program as well as their action plan to address oversight weaknesses. To assess DOD's oversight mechanisms used to safeguard the whistleblower reprisal investigative process, we reviewed key DOD guidance as well as relevant statutes and federal internal control guidance to include: the Military Whistleblower Protection Act codified at 10 U.S.C. § 1034, as amended, and DOD Directive 7050.06, *Military Whistleblower Protection* (Jul. 23, 2007); DOD Inspector General Office of the Deputy Inspector General for Investigations - Investigations Manual; GAO's *Standards for Internal Control in the Federal Government*; and the Council of the Inspectors General on Integrity and Efficiency, *Quality Standards for Investigations*, and discussed with DODIG officials their current practices. To assess DOD's adherence to its investigative process, we reviewed and discussed the DOD guidance mentioned above as well as the 1996 Inspector General Departmental Guidance (IGDG). In order to assess the completeness of DODIG's military whistleblower reprisal case files, we reviewed 91 randomly selected case files for cases closed between January 1, 2009 and March 31, 2011, (see above). To assess case file completeness, we reviewed DODIG's process, governing statute, directives, and other guidance and consulted with DODIG officials and identified 18 elements that we believe should be in case files. These 18 elements are necessary to either support the conclusions reached in the case, indicate compliance with the law or directive, or manage the case to include internal communication not specifically outlined by law or directive. The 18 elements we included for our case file review are the following:

1.	Table of Contents Sheet	10.	Interview Transcripts
2.	Database Coversheet	11.	Legal Review
3.	Investigation Oversight Worksheet	12.	Correspondence between DODIG and the Secretary of Defense regarding the final outcome of full investigations
4.	Correspondence between DODIG and the Service regarding the final outcome of the case		
		13.	Record of Corrective Action Taken
5.	Correspondence between DOD and the complainant acknowledging receipt of the complaint	14.	Army Oversight Worksheet
		15.	Correspondence between DODIG and the Secretary of Defense regarding investigations taking longer than 180 days
6.	Correspondence between DOD and the complainant informing them of the outcome of the case		
		16.	Correspondence between DODIG and the complainant regarding investigations taking longer than 180 days
7.	Investigation Analysis		
8.	Sequence of Key Events		
9.	Notification to DODIG from the Service IG that received the complaint	17.	Correspondence between DODIG and Congress acknowledging receipt of inquiry
		18.	Correspondence between DODIG and Congress informing them of the final outcome of the case

Some of these elements included specific documents. For example, the Army oversight worksheet (item 14 above) was a specific document. Other elements could be reflected in multiple documents. For example, the sequence of key events (item 8 above) could be in a larger report, be in a summary, or be its own document. Once we established the list, we further consulted with the director of DODIG's directorate responsible for conducting military whistleblower reprisal investigations to ensure that the elements selected were appropriate indicators of file completeness. The 18 elements were included in the data collection instrument and we used the methodology described above to gather information on these elements from the file. The completeness of each case file was determined individually since not all 18 elements were necessary in every case. For example, some of the 18 elements would only need to be present in a file if an investigation was conducted by a service, went beyond 180 days, or was a full investigation. We adjusted the required number of elements based on the specific circumstances of each case and calculated completeness based on that adjusted baseline. We categorized the case files as either complete (files with at least 85 percent of the case-specific elements present), partially complete (files with between 70 and 84 percent of the case-specific elements present), or incomplete (files with less than 70 percent of the case-specific elements present). To assess DODIG's monitoring of whistleblower reprisal investigations, we interviewed officials from DODIG as well as the IGs in each of the services.

In order to determine the roles and responsibilities of DODIG and the military services in providing corrective action, including the processes and procedures used by the Boards for Correction of Military Records (BCMRs) to provide relief to servicemembers who were reprised against, we reviewed applicable laws and regulations, including the Military Whistleblower Protection Act and DOD Directive 7050.06, and spoke with officials from DODIG, the service IGs, the three service BCMRs, and the Office of the Under Secretary of Defense for Personnel and Readiness – Enterprise Services. In order to determine the extent to which servicemembers with substantiated cases apply for and receive relief from the service BCMRs, we compared a list of military whistleblower reprisal claims substantiated by DODIG between fiscal year 2006 and the first half of fiscal year 2011 to information in the databases of the service BCMRs. We created the list of substantiated military whistleblower reprisal claims from the database data provided by DODIG for cases closed between fiscal year 2006 and the first half of fiscal year 2011 and created a data collection instrument. We then went to each of the three service BCMRs with a list of substantiated cases specific to each BCMR's service. BCMR officials reviewed their database and provided resultant information for each individual case, which we then recorded in the data collection instrument. We also used the data collection instrument to identify the extent to which the service BCMRs were identifying military whistleblower reprisal cases as such in their case tracking system, the processing times for such cases, and the actions taken by the BCMRs to provide remedy to the complainant. In order to determine the reliability of the data, we spoke with BCMR officials to determine how the data in their database are processed. We also reviewed the data and performed logic checks. We found that the data were sufficiently reliable for our purposes. In order to identify the extent to which DODIG was tracking the relief provided to military whistleblowers, we spoke with officials from DODIG and the service IGs. In order to determine the extent to which the services took command action against those who have reprised against military whistleblowers, we reviewed DODIG data for cases closed between fiscal year 2006 and the first half of fiscal year 2011. We also obtained information from the service IGs regarding command action for all cases closed between January 1, 2009 and March 31, 2011. We chose this time frame based on the data retention practices of the service IGs. We determined the reliability of the DODIG and service IG data on relief by comparing them and through discussions with the officials and determined that the data were not reliable enough for our purposes.

In order to describe the military reprisal caseload for the period we reviewed, we obtained a copy of data from DODIG's database using the method described above. We assessed the reliability of the data, and then coded and derived statistical output.[4] We determined some to be reliable for our purposes, including the number of closed complaints, cases closed before full investigation, and not substantiated or substantiated cases. Other data were found to be not reliable enough for our purposes because they were either inaccurate or incomplete. To obtain additional information about DODIG's caseload, we conducted a case file review of military reprisal cases using the method described above. We developed a data collection instrument and used it to record information on case characteristics located in the case files, including information about the complainant, the type of protected communication, unfavorable personnel action alleged to have occurred, and the reason for closing the case. As noted above, two analysts reviewed each case file and resolved any differences by identifying the necessary evidence in the case files.

We conducted this performance audit from April 2011 through February 2012 in accordance with generally accepted government auditing standards. Those standards require that we plan and perform the audit to obtain sufficient, appropriate evidence to provide a reasonable basis for our findings and conclusions based on our audit objectives. We believe that the evidence obtained provides a reasonable basis for our findings and conclusions based on our audit objectives.

---

[4] To assess the reliability of data elements, we performed database checks for missing fields and incorrect entries. We also verified that the investigative phases in which cases were closed (before full investigation, full investigation - not substantiated, and full investigation - substantiated) were recorded correctly through information we pulled during our case file review. We coded the data according to direction provided by agency officials at DODIG.

Appendix II: General Information on Case Characteristics for Military Whistleblower Reprisal Investigations

This appendix provides information on the characteristics of military whistleblower reprisal cases based largely on both our review of files of cases closed between January 1, 2009 and March 31, 2011, as well as data from DODIG's database for cases closed between fiscal year 2006 and the first half of fiscal year 2011.

Complainant Characteristics for Closed Cases

Generally, neither the complainants' status as officer or enlisted nor their service matched their overall proportions in the military population. For example, complaints filed by officers made up approximately 31 percent of cases closed between fiscal year 2006 and the first half of fiscal year 2011, while officers constitute approximately 16 percent of the total military population.[1] Further, servicemembers from the Air Force filed approximately 37 percent of the complaints for cases closed between fiscal year 2006 and the first half of fiscal year 2011,[2] but made up only 22 percent of the military population. Servicemembers from the Navy and Marine Corps had the fewest closed complaints during this time period— 12 percent and 1 percent, respectively, while making up 17 percent and 11 percent of the military population. The total number of closed reprisal complaints from servicemembers from the Army during this time period was higher than the other services but it was proportionate to the size of the Army. So although approximately 50 percent of military whistleblower reprisal complaints came from the Army during this time period, servicemembers from the Army also made up approximately 50 percent of the total military population. See figure 4 for a comparison of the servicemember population proportion by service compared to the proportion of reprisal cases closed.

---

[1] Percentage of closed complaints where the complainant was an officer is based on DODIG provided data for military whistleblower reprisal cases closed between fiscal year 2006 and the first half of fiscal year 2011. Note: We included the 10 percent of cases in the database that did not have data on the complainant's rank so the percentage of closed complaints from officers is at a minimum 31 percent, but could be higher. Percentage of officers in the total military population was obtained from Department of Defense, "*Defense Manpower Requirements Report – Fiscal Year 2011*" (December 2010).

[2] Figures for percentage of cases closed by complainant service exclude 1.6 percent of cases that were missing complainant service information or were coded as "Other" in DODIG's database.

Figure 4: Relative Service Size vs. Percentage of Whistleblower Complaints by Service for Cases Closed between Fiscal Year 2006 and the First Half of Fiscal Year 2011

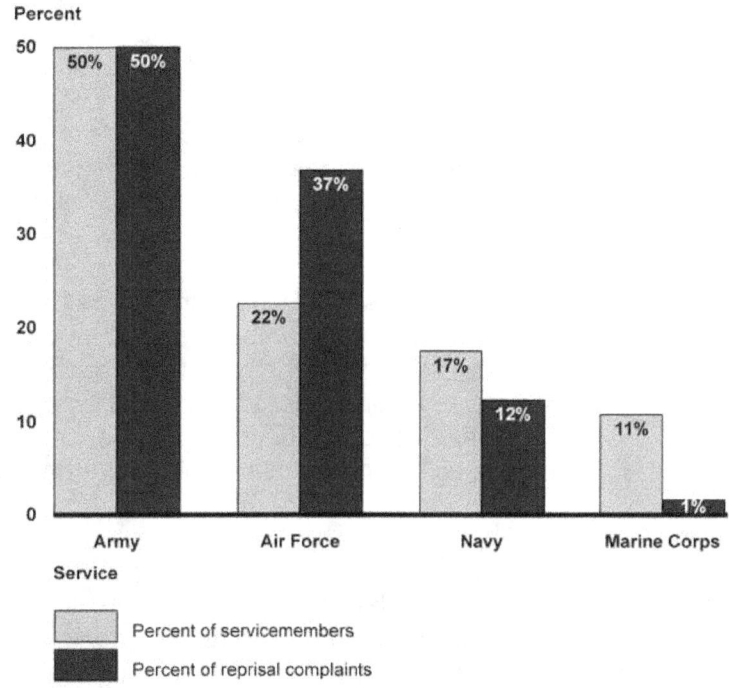

Percent

Service: Army, Air Force, Navy, Marine Corps

- Percent of servicemembers
- Percent of reprisal complaints

Source: GAO Analysis of DODIG and DOD manpower data.

Notes:

Data to determine the percent of reprisal complaints by complainant service are based on GAO analysis of DODIG data on military whistleblower reprisal cases closed between fiscal year 2006 and the first half of fiscal year 2011. We did not include 1.6 percent of cases that were missing complainant service information or were coded as "Other" in DODIG's database.

The data to determine percentage of the total servicemember population for each service come from estimated fiscal year 2011 levels contained in DOD's "Defense Manpower Requirements Report – Fiscal Year 2011" (December 2010).

Protected Communication Characteristics

According to DOD Directive 7050.06, a servicemember who makes or prepares to make a protected communication is a whistleblower. Our review of case files revealed that the primary reasons for making a protected communication are to report allegations of a violation of law or regulation (66 percent) or abuse of authority (44 percent).[3] DOD officials told us that regulations cover virtually every aspect of military life, including how to conduct personnel ratings, so complainants often cite violations of regulations in their complaints. Officials from DODIG and the service IGs also told us that the vast majority of protected communications are not about allegations of significant fraud, waste, or abuse, such as reports of unnecessarily high costs of equipment or overpayment of contracts, but rather about relatively minor issues that only impact the individual complainant, such as supervisors not following regulations regarding a performance review. Our case file review revealed that this perception is not entirely accurate. We found that approximately one-third of complaints (36 percent) were concerned solely with personal issues; one-third of complaints (33 percent) concerned fraud, waste, or abuse issues; and one-third of complaints (31 percent) were a mix of the two. The protected communications regarding allegations of fraud, waste, and abuse in the case files we reviewed tended to be about costs associated with misuse of government property, such as personal use of a government vehicle, or abuse of authority by commanders.

Unfavorable Personnel Action Characteristics

A whistleblower reprisal complaint must also include an allegation that an action was taken in reprisal against a servicemember. DOD Directive 7050.06 defines reprisal as taking or threatening to take an unfavorable personnel action, or withholding or threatening to withhold a favorable personnel action, for making or preparing to make a protected communication.[4] Based on our file review of cases closed between January 1, 2009 and March 31, 2011, the most common forms of reprisal alleged by complainants were that they received an unfavorable

---

[3] Percentages do not add up to 100 percent because complainants can allege multiple protected communications.

[4] A protected communication is any lawful communication to a Member of Congress or an IG or a communication made to certain appropriate officials that the individual reasonably believes evidences violation of law or regulation, including a law or regulation prohibiting sexual harassment or unlawful discrimination, gross mismanagement, a gross waste of funds or other resources, an abuse of authority, or a substantial and specific danger to public health or safety.

assignment or reassignment (50 percent), a poor performance evaluation (46 percent), or some sort of disciplinary action (42 percent).[5]

Reasons for Closing Cases

DODIG evaluates cases and generally closes them based on the answers to the four questions, referred to as the Acid Test (see fig. 2). Our review of randomly selected case files revealed that the most common reasons for closing a case were that DODIG determined that the complainant's actions not related to the protected communication justified the unfavorable personnel action (question 4 - 65 percent of closed cases), or that there was no unfavorable personnel action (question 2 - 41 percent of closed cases).[6] Based on our case file review, DODIG closed most complaints before conducting a full investigation and writing the resulting report of investigation (66 percent). DODIG data on cases closed between fiscal year 2006 and the first half of fiscal year 2011 show DOD closed a mean of 286 (71 percent) cases per year before conducting a full investigation, which is within the margin of error for our case file review.

Case Closure Rates

DODIG closed a mean of 405 military whistleblower reprisal cases a year between fiscal year 2006 and the first half of fiscal year 2011, ranging between a low of 325 closed cases and a high of 448 cases according to data provided by DODIG (see fig. 5).[7] We were not able to report on the military whistleblower reprisal cases received because we found that DODIG's data were not reliable for our purposes. As noted earlier, during our case file review, we observed that the case opening dates in DODIG's database did not match the opening dates documented in the case files. Without data on when cases were opened, we were unable to compare case opening and closure rates and determine if more cases were being opened or closed in any given year. Although we found the DODIG data to be reliable enough for our purposes in reporting total cases closed in a

---

[5] Percentages reported on reprisal types do not add up to 100 percent because complainants often allege multiple reprisal types.

[6] Percentages reported on reasons for closing cases do not add up to 100 percent because one complaint often includes multiple allegations and investigators often cite multiple reasons for closing a case.

[7] Our data for fiscal year 2011 go only through the first half of that year. Assuming the total number of cases for the second half were similar to the 194 cases closed in the first half, fiscal year 2011 totals would fall within the range noted.

year, these figures do not match the data reported by DODIG in its semiannual reports to Congress. Those figures include more than military whistleblower reprisal cases, but adjusting for these additional cases does not fully make up the discrepancy between the figures in the semiannual reports and the data provided to us by DODIG. DODIG officials were not certain of the exact cause for the discrepancy and said that they did not have auditable data for their semiannual report figures for the time period we examined.

Figure 5: Number of Closed Cases between Fiscal Year 2006 and the First Half of Fiscal Year 2011

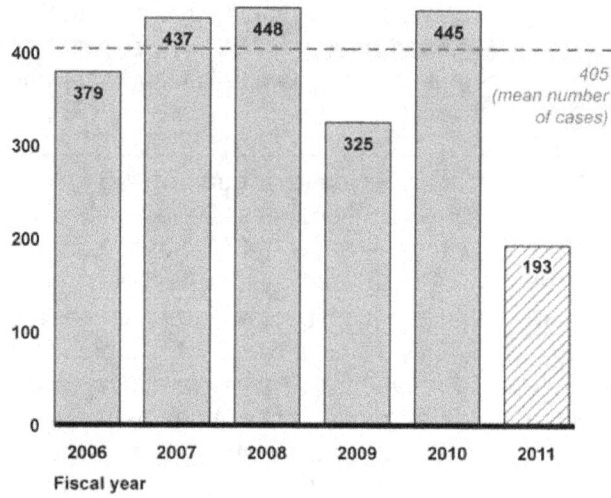

Number of cases

Source: GAO analysis of DODIG data between FY2006 and the first half of FY2011.

Note:

Fiscal year 2011 numbers reflect cases closed between October 1, 2010 and March 31, 2011.

Full Investigation and Substantiation Rates

Our analysis of DODIG data on military whistleblower reprisal cases closed between fiscal year 2006 through the first half of fiscal year 2011 shows that DOD fully investigated a mean of 119 cases a year (29 percent of all cases), with 25 of those full investigations substantiated (6 percent of all cases), and 94 of those full investigations not substantiated (23 percent of all cases). DODIG determined that a mean of 286 cases a year (71 percent of all cases) did not warrant full investigation over the time period we reviewed. The number of full investigations ranged from a high of 156 in fiscal years 2006 and 2007 to a low of 69 in fiscal year 2009 and the number of substantiated cases ranged from a high of 40 in fiscal year 2006 to a low of 12 in fiscal year 2009 for cases closed during this time period.[8] Further, the number of full investigations and substantiated cases closed during this time period tended to be higher in the earlier fiscal years than the later fiscal years, with fiscal year 2009 being the lowest for both. Figure 6 shows the total cases closed by investigative phase for each fiscal year.

---

[8] Our data for fiscal year 2011 go only through the first half of that year. Assuming the number of fully investigated and substantiated cases for the second half were similar to the 52 fully investigated and 10 substantiated cases closed in the first half, fiscal year 2011 totals would fall within the ranges noted.

Figure 6: Comparison of Substantiated, Not Substantiated, and Cases Not Fully Investigated for Military Whistleblower Reprisal Cases Closed between Fiscal Year 2006 and the First Half of Fiscal Year 2011

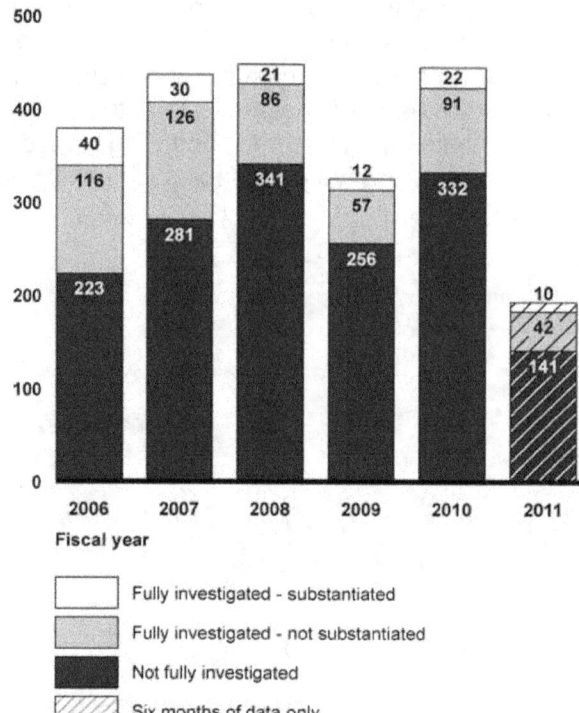

Source: GAO analysis of DODIG data between FY2006 and the first half of FY2011.

Note:

Data include two Army cases closed in fiscal year 2006 that were inappropriately coded in DODIG's database as substantiated military whistleblower reprisal cases.

Further, the mean number of military whistleblower reprisal cases closed per year over this time period along with the number of cases fully investigated and substantiated varied by investigating organization according to data provided by DODIG. For example, the Army closed the highest number of cases per year (158 cases per year) and the Marine Corps closed the fewest cases per year (4 cases per year) over this time period.[9] The Air Force fully investigated the most cases per year (46 cases per year) and the Marine Corps fully investigated the fewest cases per year (2 cases per year) between fiscal year 2006 and the first half of fiscal year 2011. The Air Force and the Army substantiated the most cases per year (10 cases per year each) during this time period. The Marine Corps and DODIG substantiated the fewest cases per year (1 case per year each) over this time period. See figure 7 for the mean yearly number of closed cases by investigative phase and investigating organization for fiscal year 2006 through the first half of fiscal year 2011.

---

[9] The numbers reported in this paragraph may not match those reported in fig. 7 due to rounding of each investigative phase number in fig. 7.

Figure 7: Mean Yearly Number of Closed Cases by Phase of Investigation and Investigating Organization between Fiscal Year 2006 and the First Half of Fiscal Year 2011

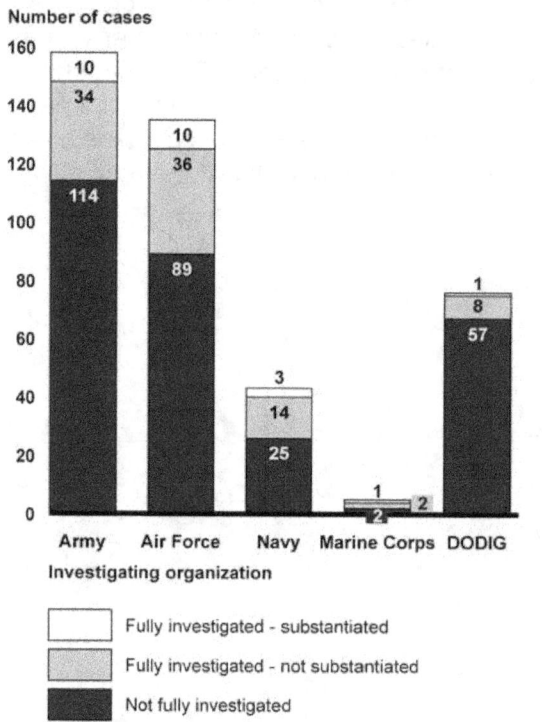

Source: GAO analysis of DODIG data between FY2006 and the first half of FY2011.

Notes:

Mean total number of cases for the Navy and Marine Corps do not match table 2 due to rounding.

Data presented here do not include seven cases closed over this time period where DODIG data for investigating organization is missing or listed as "Joint" or "Other."

Data include two Army cases closed in fiscal year 2006 that were inappropriately coded in DODIG's database as substantiated military whistleblower reprisal cases.

The percentage of total cases that are fully investigated and substantiated has generally declined between fiscal year 2006 and the first half of fiscal year 2011, reaching its lowest point in both cases in fiscal year 2009. Figure 8 shows the variation in the percentage of closed cases fully

investigated by processing organization.[10] DODIG's full investigation rate
was lowest during this time period and it, along with the Air Force, had a
generally steady full investigation rate whereas the Army and Navy full
investigation rate generally declined over this time period.

**Figure 8: Percentage of Full Investigations out of Total Closed Investigations by
Investigating Organization**

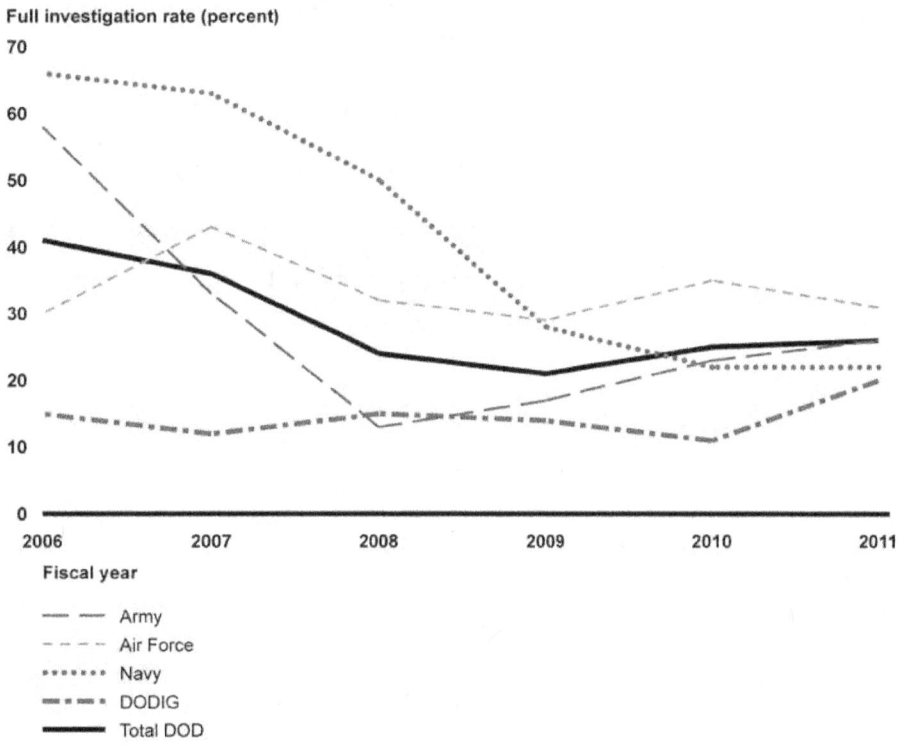

Full investigation rate (percent)

Fiscal year

— — Army
– – – Air Force
••••••• Navy
■ ■ ■ ■ DODIG
———— Total DOD

Source: GAO analysis of DODIG data between FY2006 and the first half of FY2011.

Notes:

Fiscal year 2011 numbers reflect cases closed between October 1, 2010 and March 31, 2011.

Marine Corps data were not shown due to the low number of cases closed and high variation in rates.
Marine Corps data were included in the total.

---

[10] For both figs. 8 and 9 we did not include the data for the Marine Corps because the low
number of cases processed by the Marine Corps caused small variations in the number of
cases fully investigated and substantiated to show up as large percentage variations. The
Marine Corps data were included in the totals in both figures.

Data presented here do not include seven cases closed over this time period where DODIG data for investigating organization are missing or listed as "Joint" or "Other."

Data include two Army cases closed in fiscal year 2006 that were inappropriately coded in DODIG's database as substantiated military whistleblower reprisal cases.

Figure 9 also shows the variation by processing organization in the percentage of closed cases substantiated over this time period. In general, the substantiation rate declined, with DODIG having the lowest substantiation rate. However, there was some variation in the rate for each processing organization. Excluding the Marine Corps (see footnote 10), the Navy was the organization with the most variation, with substantiation rates ranging from 2 percent to 16 percent. DODIG was the organization with the least variation, with substantiation rates ranging from 0 percent to 3 percent.

Figure 9: Percentage of Substantiated Investigations Out of Total Closed Investigations by Investigating Organization

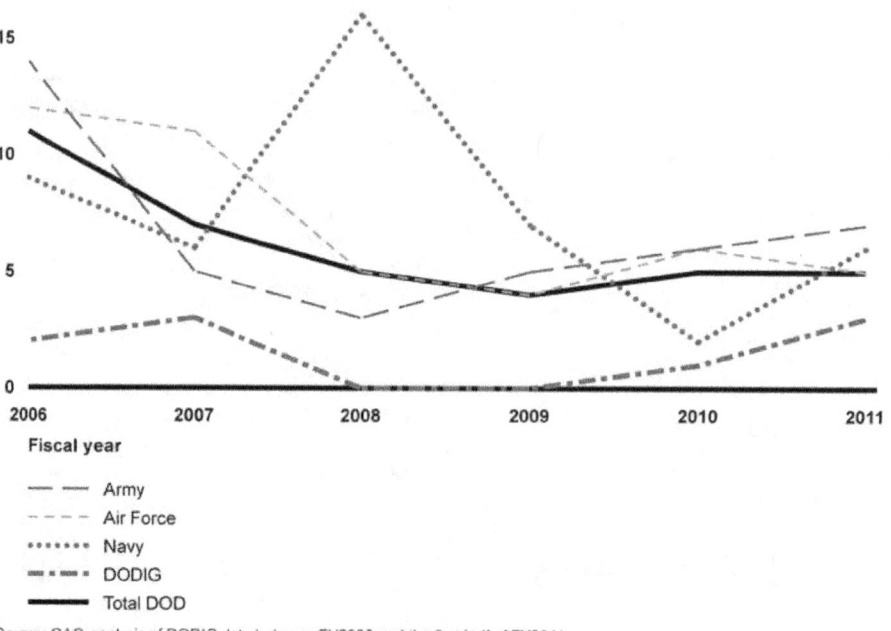

Source: GAO analysis of DODIG data between FY2006 and the first half of FY2011.

Notes:

Fiscal year 2011 numbers reflect cases closed between October 1, 2010 and March 31, 2011.

Marine Corps data were not shown due to the low number of cases closed and high variation in rates. Marine Corps data were included in the total.

Data presented here do not include seven cases closed over this time period where DODIG data for investigating organization are missing or listed as "Joint" or "Other."

Data include two Army cases closed in fiscal year 2006 that were inappropriately coded in DODIG's database as substantiated military whistleblower reprisal cases.

Appendix III: Comparison of Whistleblower Reprisal Cases That Were and Were Not Identified as Reprisal by Service BCMRs

	Number of cases (percent)		Mean days to close case		Cases over 180 days (percent)		Remedy provided (percent)	
All cases								
Air Force	9		256		4		9	
Army	6		167		2		3	
Navy (all)	10		118		3		8	
Navy		9		93		2		8
Marine Corps		1		338		1		0
Total	**25**		**179**		**9 (36%)**		**20 (80%)**	
Cases identified as reprisal								
Air Force	4		230		2		4	
Army	5		166		2		3	
Navy (all)	6		40		0		5	
Navy		6		40		0		5
Marine Corps		0		—		—		—
Total	**15 (60%)**		**133**		**4 (27%)**		**12 (80%)**	
Cases not identified as reprisal								
Air Force	5		277		2		5	
Army	1		168		0		0	
Navy (all)	4		235		3		3	
Navy		3		200		2		3
Marine Corps		1		253		1		0
Total	**10 (40%)**		**249**		**5 (50%)**		**8 (80%)**	

Source: GAO analysis of DOD information.

Notes:

Based on DODIG data for cases that included military whistleblower reprisal allegations substantiated by DODIG between October 1, 2005 and March 31, 2011, and BCMR data regarding the cases submitted to them, including case outcomes.

Data do not include cases in which, according to DODIG data, the military whistleblower reprisal allegations are not substantiated but an improper referral for mental health evaluation (IMHE) is substantiated.

The Navy BCMR reviews cases for the Department of the Navy and therefore handles cases from both Navy personnel and Marine Corps personnel.

Two Navy BCMR cases—one from the Marine Corps and one from the Navy—were included and considered as not having received remedy although the Navy BCMR data are unclear whether or not it provided remedy. The Marine Corps case was not identified by the Navy BCMR as being a military whistleblower reprisal case. The Navy case was identified as a military whistleblower reprisal case.

Remedy provided indicates that the complainant received at least partial remedy. It does not indicate that the complainant received the exact remedy they were seeking.

Appendix IV: Comments from the Department of Defense

INSPECTOR GENERAL
DEPARTMENT OF DEFENSE
4800 MARK CENTER DRIVE
ALEXANDRIA, VIRGINIA 22350-1500

FEB 1 7 2012

Ms. Zina D. Merritt, Director
Defense Capabilities Management
U.S. Government Accountability Office
441 G Street, NW
Washington, DC 20548

Dear Ms. Merritt:

This is the response to the GAO Draft Report, GAO-12-362, "WHISTLEBLOWER PROTECTION: Actions Needed to Improve DOD's Military Whistleblower Reprisal Program," dated February 2012 (GAO Code 351599).

Recommendations 1, 2, 3 and 5 are directed to the Department of Defense Inspector General (DoD IG). The DoD IG concurs with comment with the recommendations. Recommendation 4 is directed to the Secretary of Defense. The DoD concurs with comment with the recommendation. Detailed responses to each recommendation are enclosed.

As acknowledged in your report, the DoD IG has embarked on an aggressive path forward to realize our vision of being the model whistleblower protection program not only in the Department of Defense, but also in the Federal government. To that end, the DoD IG has increased the resources dedicated to the whistleblower protection program and has asked the Secretaries of the Military Services to favorably consider requests from their respective Inspectors General for additional resources.

Over the past year, the DoD IG has been actively engaged in keeping Congress fully informed on the DoD whistleblower reprisal investigation program through testimony, briefings, and the Semiannual Report to Congress. The DoD IG will ensure that information on the timeliness of investigations is provided to Congress.

The DoD IG has also taken significant measures to improve the transparency and the integrity of the data relating to whistleblower investigations. These measures include implementing immediate improvements to legacy information management systems, while simultaneously pursuing the acquisition of the next generation technology. Technology enhancements will provide capability to the DoD IG to improve the tracking and analysis of the whistleblower investigations process and to implement policies and procedures to measure and improve investigation timelines.

2

Thank you for the opportunity to review the report. If you have any questions regarding these comments, please contact me at (703) 604-8324.

Sincerely,

John Crane
Assistant Inspector General
Communications and Congressional Liaison

Enclosure

**RESPONSE TO GAO DRAFT REPORT, GAO-12-362,
"WHISTLEBLOWER PROTECTION: ACTIONS NEEDED TO IMPROVE
DOD'S MILITARY WHISTLEBLOWER REPRISAL PROGRAM,"
DATED FEBRUARY 2012
(GAO CODE 351599)**

RECOMMENDATION 1. The GAO recommends that the Secretary of Defense work in coordination with DODIG to:

- Implement policies and procedures to ensure accurate and complete recording and consistent tracking of total case processing time and processing time for various phases of the investigation;
- Track and analyze timeliness data to identify reforms that could aid in processing cases within the 180 days provided by law; and
- Regularly report to Congress on the timeliness of military whistleblower reprisal investigations, including the number of cases exceeding the 180 days provided by law. DODIG could do so in its semi-annual reports.

DoD IG RESPONSE. Concur. The DoD IG recognizes that policies and procedures are needed to ensure accurate and complete tracking of processing time for all phases of administrative investigations. As a result, the Deputy Inspector General for Administrative Investigations (DIG-AI) has modified internal processes to minimize delays in initiating and completing investigations, and is updating policy manuals to support and enforce this goal. The DIG-AI is also working to redesign the current case management database for administrative investigations to better capture and report crucial timeliness-related information. The redesigned database should be ready to launch within the third quarter of FY 2012, and DoD IG will rely on data analysis to evaluate its current reforms and identify further changes that may be needed to meet the 180-day requirement. In addition, DoD IG will report information on timeliness to Congress.

RECOMMENDATION 2. The GAO recommends that the Secretary of Defense work in coordination with DODIG to:

- Develop and implement performance metrics to ensure the quality and effectiveness of the investigative process, such as ensuring that the case files contain evidence sufficient to support the conclusions;
- Update whistleblower reprisal investigative guidance and ensure that it is consistently followed. This should include clarifying reporting requirements, responsibilities and terminology; and,
- Consistently monitor the status of whistleblower reprisal investigations.

DODIG should work in concert with the service IGs when implementing these recommendations.

DoD IG RESPONSE. Concur. DoD IG is currently revising its manual for administrative investigations to include clearly defined performance metrics for all aspects of investigations, the required contents of investigative case files, as well as defining reporting requirements, responsibilities, and relevant terminology. Moreover, the DIG-AI has established a new oversight team which reviews and approves the determinations reached by the Service IGs on complaints handled by the Services, and is also currently establishing procedures by which they will directly monitor the progress of investigations and track command actions taken on substantiated complaints of reprisal.

RECOMMENDATION 3. The GAO recommends that the Secretary of Defense work in coordination with DODIG to identify best practices and develop the necessary processes and procedures to ensure that all whistleblower reprisal allegations substantiated by DODIG are considered under the whistleblower statute by the appropriate service BCMR. For example, DODIG could provide more detailed recommendations regarding corrective action for the complainant. DODIG should work in close consultation with the service IGs and the BCMRs when implementing this recommendation.

DoD IG RESPONSE. Concur. Within the next six weeks, DoD IG will meet with the Service IGs and BCMRs to begin identifying best practices and developing an effective way forward.

RECOMMENDATION 4. The GAO recommends that the Secretary of Defense direct the secretaries of the military departments take action to ensure that military whistleblower cases are correctly identified and processed by the BCMRs. Such actions could include modifying the form used to apply to the BCMR; additional training so that BCMR staff can better identify cases; or developing methods for identifying cases for which the BCMRs have received DODIG substantiated case notifications.

DoD RESPONSE. Concur. This issue will be included in the consideration of best practices and a way forward described in response to Recommendation 3, above. Specifically, BCMRs will consider how best to ensure that whistleblowers whose reprisal complaints are substantiated are provided with all the information they need to determine if an application to a BCMR is appropriate in their specific cases.

RECOMMENDATION 5. The GAO recommends that the Secretary of Defense work in coordination with DODIG to:

- Establish standardized corrective action reporting requirements;
- Consistently track and regularly reconcile data regarding corrective action; and

- Regularly report to Congress on the frequency and type of corrective action taken in response to substantiated reprisal claims. DODIG could do so in its semi-annual reports to Congress.

DODIG should work in concert with the service IGs and BCMRs when implementing these recommendations.

DoD IG RESPONSE. Concur. The redesigned case management database for Administrative Investigations will enable the DoD IG to document in detail both corrective actions taken to remedy reprisal actions and disciplinary actions taken against those who were responsible for the substantiated reprisals. The DIG-AI will thus be able to provide data in far greater detail to Congress on the frequency and type of action taken when reprisal is substantiated. The procedure for tracking command action by the DoD IG begins with a request, in the letter notifying the Service Secretary of the substantiation of a claim, that the Service inform DoD IG within 60 days of their transmittal memorandum of any corrective action taken. If DoD IG has not received notification of the corrective action within 60 days, they ask the Service IG to follow up with the Service and report back to DoD IG. If, after 90 days have passed since the transmittal of the findings, DoD IG still has not heard, they ask again. DoD IG continues to follow up every 30 days with the Service IG until they have confirmed what action the Service has taken in response to a substantiated reprisal investigation.

Appendix V: GAO Contacts and Staff Acknowledgments

GAO Contacts

Zina D. Merritt, (202) 512- 5257 or merrittz@gao.gov

Staff Acknowledgments

In addition to the contact named above, Assistant Director Marie Mak, Joanna Chan, Nicolaas Cornelisse, Justin Fisher, Julia Kennon, K. Nicole Willems, Michael Silver, Sheena Smith, Amie Steele, Emily Suarez-Harris, and Erik Wilkins-McKee made major contributions to this report.

GAO's Mission	The Government Accountability Office, the audit, evaluation, and investigative arm of Congress, exists to support Congress in meeting its constitutional responsibilities and to help improve the performance and accountability of the federal government for the American people. GAO examines the use of public funds; evaluates federal programs and policies; and provides analyses, recommendations, and other assistance to help Congress make informed oversight, policy, and funding decisions. GAO's commitment to good government is reflected in its core values of accountability, integrity, and reliability.
Obtaining Copies of GAO Reports and Testimony	The fastest and easiest way to obtain copies of GAO documents at no cost is through GAO's website (www.gao.gov). Each weekday afternoon, GAO posts on its website newly released reports, testimony, and correspondence. To have GAO e-mail you a list of newly posted products, go to www.gao.gov and select "E-mail Updates."
Order by Phone	The price of each GAO publication reflects GAO's actual cost of production and distribution and depends on the number of pages in the publication and whether the publication is printed in color or black and white. Pricing and ordering information is posted on GAO's website, http://www.gao.gov/ordering.htm.
	Place orders by calling (202) 512-6000, toll free (866) 801-7077, or TDD (202) 512-2537.
	Orders may be paid for using American Express, Discover Card, MasterCard, Visa, check, or money order. Call for additional information.
Connect with GAO	Connect with GAO on Facebook, Flickr, Twitter, and YouTube. Subscribe to our RSS Feeds or E-mail Updates. Listen to our Podcasts. Visit GAO on the web at www.gao.gov.
To Report Fraud, Waste, and Abuse in Federal Programs	Contact: Website: www.gao.gov/fraudnet/fraudnet.htm E-mail: fraudnet@gao.gov Automated answering system: (800) 424-5454 or (202) 512-7470
Congressional Relations	Katherine Siggerud, Managing Director, siggerudk@gao.gov, (202) 512-4400, U.S. Government Accountability Office, 441 G Street NW, Room 7125, Washington, DC 20548
Public Affairs	Chuck Young, Managing Director, youngc1@gao.gov, (202) 512-4800 U.S. Government Accountability Office, 441 G Street NW, Room 7149 Washington, DC 20548

Please Print on Recycled Paper.

www.ingramcontent.com/pod-product-compliance
Lightning Source LLC
Chambersburg PA
CBHW081134290526
45795CB00006B/2232